Sea-Guides by H. M. Denham

THE AEGEAN
THE ADRIATIC
THE IONIAN ISLANDS TO RHODES
SOUTHERN TURKEY, THE LEVANT AND CYPRUS
THE TYRRHENIAN SEA

THE TYRRHENIAN SEA
A SEA-GUIDE TO ITS COASTS
AND ISLANDS

THE
TYRRHENIAN SEA

A Sea-Guide to its
Coasts and Islands

H. M. DENHAM

W · W · NORTON & COMPANY · INC·
New York

Acknowledgements

I am grateful to Lord Merthyr, Mr. Peter Edwards, Mr. John Burgess and my Italian friends who have cruised in their yachts in the Tyrrhenian Sea, all of whom have helped me with additional information.

My thanks are also due to my wife for her line drawings and help with the text; to Miss Shirley Deane for advice with her intimate knowledge of Corsica and once more to Mrs. Jehane West for geographical and historical data.

ISLANDS and COASTLINE
of the TYRRHENIAN SEA

ITALY

2

1

CORSICA

Bonifacio Strait

3

T Y R R H E N I A N

S E A

6

SARDINIA

4

Lipari Is.

Ustica

Aegadean Is.

SICILY

5

Pantelleria

Diagram of Chapters

Contents

Illustrations

Preface

The Tyrrhenian Sea was a name originally given by the Greeks to the waters bordering the west coast of Italy, where the Tyrrhenoi (known to the Romans as Tusci or Etrusci) had settled and built their towns. According to Herodotus they originated by the Aegean Sea in Lydia, Asia Minor. Today the Tyrrhenian Sea is the large area enclosed by the Tuscan Islands in the north, Corsica and Sardinia in the west and Sicily in the south.

During the sailing season the weather in this area is very agreeable: according to Sailing Directions, during average summer months winds from a N.W. direction predominate, blowing mostly with a strength of force 1 to 3 and seldom more than 4 or 5. In the early part of August there is usually a disturbing week of bad weather before it again settles.

Most people are under the impression that one must go as far as the Adriatic or Aegean to find unspoilt and attractive anchorages, but a thorough exploration of all the Tyrrhenian Sea has to offer will show that this is not so. This book describes not only the shores and islands bordering the Tyrrhenian Sea, but also embraces the west coasts of Corsica and Sardinia, as well as the whole seaboard of Sicily and the nearby islands. Each of these islands is very different from its neighbour, and approaching by sea one observes the contrast even more. For example, when sighting the tall island of Corsica the mountain chains stand out with a sharpness of form more magnificent than anywhere in the Western Mediterranean. For volcanoes one must go to Vesuvius on the mainland, to Etna in Sicily, or to the smaller islands of Stromboli and Vulcano. The Bonifacio Strait with northern Sardinia provides some of the most fascinating anchorages and Sicily has its Greek temples, Romanesque cathedrals and mosaics.

The lesser islands are mostly in groups, the Tuscan Islands being the most important. There are the Aegadean and the Lipari or Aeolean, the Pontine groups, and individual islands such as Ischia, Capri and Ustica. All are different from one another, physically, architecturally and in the character and occupations of the people. Two thousand years of history have left their mark almost everywhere.

The harbours and coves on most islands provide sufficient shelter and facilities for a yacht; but even where they are sometimes inadequate, shore excursions to places of interest can usually be made from the nearest safe port.

GENERAL INFORMATION

Spelling of Names. Normally place names are spelt as in the country to which they belong, but for convenience certain exceptions are made where English titles are generally in use, e.g. Naples (Napoli) Aeolean Islands (Isoli Aeoli).

Formalities. In 1967 there was no formality about entering the French ports mentioned in this book. In the case of Italian ports, however, a yacht on entering the first major port is issued with a *Constituto* (*Constituto in arrivo per il naviglio da diporto*). On this form are entered the yacht's particulars and details of the crew. At each subsequent port it should be produced and if necessary taken to the Harbour Office to be stamped.

Fuel, Water, Food and Drink.

(a) Fuel can sometimes be obtained from a waterside pump, but more often has to be carried in a container from a nearby garage. In certain French ports one may be able to get fuel from a fisherman's pump at a reduced price. In Italy diesel fuel is expensive except for large yachts requiring big quantities which are obtainable out of bond through the Customs.

(b) Water can be obtained through the Harbour Authority at most ports and is sold inexpensively at varying prices. In hot weather it may be highly chlorinated.

(c) Food and Wine are described under the heading of each country.

Health. In July, August and early September the places described in this book have hot climates and one should take certain precautions; wash fruit with a few grains of permanganate of potash in the water, examine vegetables against intrusion of cockroaches etc. A well stocked medicine-chest such as that recommended by Yachting World Diary should be carried on board.

Charts and Sailing Directions referred to in this book are British Admiralty Charts and the Sailing Directions are Vol. I and Vol. II of the *Mediterranean Pilot*. Both French and Italian charts can be bought at major naval ports, but it is considered that British charts are adequate and usually more practical.

The Italian book *Mari e Porti* which has just been published shows small plans of certain ports which are not printed on British charts. References to it in this book are indicated as *M. & P.* Soundings are shown in metres on Italian charts, a procedure now being followed on British Admiralty charts.

Weather for local areas is explained at the beginning of each chapter. Forecasts are given on the following transmissions:

(a) *Corsica*—Monte Carlo Radio in French

1,400 metres at 07.02 hours

205 metres at 11.58 hours

49.5 metres at 17.58 hours

206 metres at 21.02 hours

(b) *The Italian coast and islands*—A powerful broadcasting station transmits on 1,034 kc/s a good weather forecast (*Bullettino per Navigare*) in dictation speed at:

06.25, 15.00 (18.40 on Sundays) and 21.55

It is easy to follow the Italian vocabulary since it is not wide and many words are similar in English. The broadcast follows this pattern:

Gale warnings (*Avviso*) which include winds of Force 7 and over. A frequent phrase is '*Temporale con locale colpi di vento*'—thunderstorms with gale-force gusts locally.

The general situation (*Situazione*)—depressions, fronts etc.

A forecast for each sea area or group of sea areas:

> Direction and strength of wind
> Sea, on the Beaufort Scale
> Sky—clear (*sereno*); cloudy (*nuvoloso*) overcast (*coperto*)
> Visibility

Further outlook.

(c) *Malta Radio*—a coastal station, gives a weather forecast on 2,625 kc/s at 10.03 and 18.03 G.M.T., but it covers only the immediate Malta area.

For Yacht Repairs and Laying-up in the Tyrrhenian Sea a popular yacht yard is at Porto Santo Stefano—*Cantiere Navale dell'Argentario*. Malta has recently become important and attracts about 300 yachts for laying-up in winter. The marina and repair facilities at these ports are described in Chapter 7.

Along all these coasts one notices certain things in common:

The Watch Towers, to be seen on many headlands or sometimes overlooking a small cove, were built to warn and protect villagers or shipping in the anchorage against the depredations of Barbary pirates. Many were kept manned even after Nelson's time.

Local Craft. The two types of craft to be seen during recent centuries have now almost disappeared from the Tyrrhenian Sea. Sails have all been replaced by motor; only steadying-sails are used and modern hulls are often built for fishermen to suit power propulsion:

The *tartane* is a vessel usually of about 40 tons burthen with a pronounced sheer, clipper bow, and pointed stern. The vessels are mostly half-decked with hatch covers and some are open boats. The rig is a single lateen often with one or two jibs. These boats although hardly ever under sail nowadays can still sometimes be seen carrying wine, salt, coral, fish and mixed cargoes over short distances in the coastal trade of Sardinia and Sicily.

The sketch shows a *tartane* built at the end of the last century when she normally carried a topsail. These sails went out when motors were fitted and have rarely been seen for many years.

The *felucca* which went out early in the century was of two types: The coastal passenger-boat with a lug- or lateen-sail and manned by 4 or 6 oarsmen, was used only for short day trips and has now disappeared. The larger type, sometimes rigged as a 3-masted lateen schooner, had a *tartane*-like hull often of 100 tons burthen. Although copied both by Spain and Turkey no more are to be seen.

The fishing boats and *tartanes* today have an unusual custom in common during bad weather in port. When possible the smaller boats haul up on the beach; but the larger ones lie at moorings awaiting the storm, abandoned by their crews. Not one man remains on board to act in emergency. This is on account of insurance conditions, for the underwriters maintain that if a man is left on board he might take fright at the violence of the storm, cut the cable and allow the vessel to drive ashore.

A few traditional types of small fishing boats have survived in certain Sicilian ports and are still in service today. Some unusual features are probably of Arab origin; those at Trapani and Porticello are described under the port heading.

Although Malta is outside the scope of this book, except as a laying-up and refitting port as described in Chapter 7, its traditional local craft still survive, and deserve a brief description:

The Gozo Boats, with two lateen sails, are gaudily painted craft with pronounced sheer, about 40 feet long—an elongated stem and high stern-post. The turtle decking forward and aft, and the numerable wash boards were all features peculiar to the Gozo boat which, until after the First World War, plied regularly between Malta and Gozo carrying passengers and vegetables between the two islands.

ELBA AND THE TUSCAN ISLANDS
AND ADJACENT MAINLAND COAST

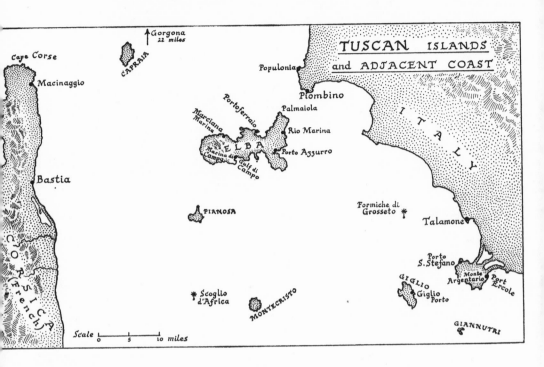

Island of Elba
  Porto Ferraio
  Rio Marina
  Porto Azzurro
  Marina di Campo
  Marciana Marina
Island of Pianosa
Island of Gorgona
Island of Capraia
Island of Montecristo
Island of Giglio
Island of Giannutri

MAINLAND COAST
Piombino
Forno Cove
Talamone
Porto Santo Stefano
Porto Ercole

I

Elba and the Tuscan Islands and Adjacent Mainland Coast

THE TUSCAN ISLANDS

The Tuscan Islands which straddle the sea between Italy and Corsica have become known to foreigners only in recent years because of the importance of Elba. But Giglio is also attractive, with a small port, lying close off the mainland peninsula of Argentario; the remaining five islands, each different in character from its neighbour, have scarcely been visited by yachts. This is because circumstances prevented it, for two islands were prisons: one a royal shooting preserve, another privately owned, and the last one (Pianosa) so sparsely populated and uninteresting that no one wants to go there.

Elba has nearly half a dozen ports affording varying degrees of shelter; Giglio's port is well sheltered and so is Capraia's; but except for the convict island of Gorgona with its small shallow harbour, the other three islands are without a sheltered anchorage. Although Elba and possibly Giglio are of outstanding attraction, nevertheless a brief visit by a yacht to the other islands should not be missed.

Pilotage Information is given in *Mediterranean Pilot*, Vol. II.

Elba is a delightful island to visit in a yacht. The small towns and villages, the ports and anchorages all make an individual appeal. Even in the hottest weather the slopes and valleys are always refreshingly green.

Centuries before Roman times Elba was important for the iron mines, but when France, Spain and the Italian duchies became political rivals in the 17th and 18th centuries the harbours became more important than the ore. Although Elba was normally under the suzerainty of the Duchy of Tuscany, at the end of the 18th century Britain seized the island for two years, and shortly afterwards Elba provided a temporary kingdom for the exiled Emperor Napoleon. Having changed rulers again she finally became part of the new United Italy in 1862, and under this government she has since remained.

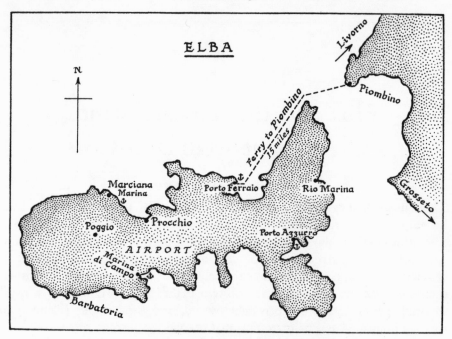

> 'Every man and vessel safely moored in Porto
> Ferraio, for its size the most complete harbour
> in the world.' NELSON, 1796

Porto Ferraio the capital of Elba, has one of the most secure harbours in the Mediterranean.

Approach. Chart 1719, plan. The harbour is easy to enter day or night.

Berth. Stern to the quay anywhere convenient at the S.E. side of the basin.

Facilities. Many shops in the vicinity, also hotels, bars and restaurants. Water is laid on at the quay, fuel at pumps S.E. of the port (sufficient depth alongside for medium-draught yachts); a laundry at the quayside. Daily ferry steamer to Piombino, many services in summer, also hydrofoil connection with Livorno and Capraia. Air service to Milan.

Close behind the quays at the port is the Piazza della Republica with its pleasant 18th-century architecture and typical pediments of the period. Here one should choose one of the several restaurants and dine on the terrace in the atmosphere of the past.

One must also climb up the old fortifications to see the splendid view of the port. The present town of Porto Ferraio and the two commanding forts date back to the 16th century when Cosimo I, Duke of Florence, turned the harbour into an important trading centre. High above the harbour, and having the finest view across the bay, stands the Palazzino dei Mulini, the main residence of Napoleon during his exile on the island.

The strategic importance of Ferraio was appreciated by rival Mediterranean powers, especially its use as a fleet base to ward off foreign invaders wishing to descend upon the mainland ports of Tuscany. When the British seized Porto

Ferraio, Nelson's ships used to come here to careen, to take in water, and to embark stores; but after a couple of years it had to be abandoned and once more possession of the island was in dispute.

Fifteen years later, when the people had just learnt that the long Napoleonic campaign had ended, a surprise awaited them. In April, H.M.S. *Undaunted* unexpectedly entered Porto Ferraio with the exiled Napoleon on board; he had been appointed King of Elba by the victorious allies. After only ten months on the throne Napoleon had planned his escape, and embarking in his brig *Inconstant* (300 tons) on 26th February, 1815, he successfully evaded Allied patrols, and reached the French coast three days later.

The harbour today can be very congested with yachts. The ferry-pier and the hydrofoil landing-quay have been moved outside, westward of the port, where modern buildings and shops are also springing up. In hot weather it is refreshing to go across to Cala Bagnaia, one mile eastward, where one may anchor, somewhat insecurely, off the bathing beach.

Cruising southward down the east coast of Elba one notices the irregular nature of the green mountain slopes—the patches of brown ore are evidence of nearly three thousand years of iron mining. The tips and piers at sheltered indentations along the coast show where small ore ships and an occasional ferry still call. Today the ore deposits are nearly exhausted and most of the work is now devoted to extracting more ore from the rubble left behind by the ancients. This sometimes involves work on the beaches when, after a hard onshore wind, the sea may become discoloured with a strong yellow-brown stain for many miles along the coast.

Rio Marina is Elba's old iron-ore village, close to the workings, with a small port beneath, of little interest to a yacht.

Approach and berth. Chart 3905. Berth stern to the quay in the S.E. corner, or one can sometimes lie alongside at the S. or E. side in 10-feet depths, open to N.E. The ferry berths at the outer end of the breakwater.

The authorities are now trying to attract tourists, but Rio Marina seems unlikely to become a rival to the more popular places on the island.

Porto Azzurro. A picturesque little port with a village lying in a magnificent mountainous setting—rather overpowered by tourism in recent years.

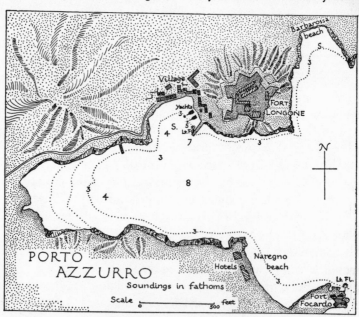

Approach. Chart 1719, plan. There is no difficulty day or night, although in darkness care should be taken to avoid hitting the steamer's hauling-off buoy, 20 yards N. of the molehead.

Berth. The north corner of the harbour has been dredged to accommodate the larger yachts which can berth in the normal way stern to the quay, but owing to quay space required for steamers little room is left for the yachts. [See photograph facing p. 32.]

Facilities. At the N. and E. quays fresh water is now laid on. There are a number of shops, hotels and restaurants, for the place now caters for package tours. Many people bathe from the sandy beach inside the harbour; but it is usually clean enough to swim off some steps at the end of the breakwater. There is daily steamer communication with Piombino.

The great fortress of Longone, built in the middle of the 16th century by Santa Cruz, formerly Spanish Viceroy at Naples, was overcome by the French a few years later and greatly strengthened. Nevertheless it was contested again and again by both French and Pisans. On reverting to Italy in the last century it became a prison—notorious for its criminals. Subsequently the village began to grow up by the waterfront, and this century saw the sea walls built to protect the buildings from the winter gales. The possibility of tourism came to be realized, but the name Longone, which for so many years had been associated with unfortunate prisoners, brought a feeling of gloom to potential tourists in Italy and therefore the name was changed. Azzurro has certainly proved a successful choice, and today hotels may be seen standing above many of the more attractive bathing beaches around this large inlet. Close outside the village are vineyards which produce a dry or semi-dry white wine that can be bought on draught.

Marina di Campo, once a small fishing village, has recently acquired a modern quarter mainly given over to tourism. The port formed by two short moles is suitable only for very small yachts.

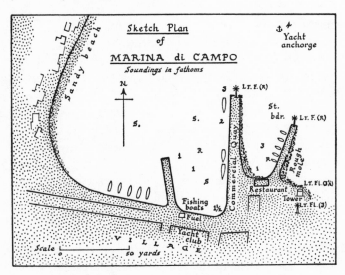

Approach. Chart 3905. The small port is protected by a short outer mole extending in a N.N.E. direction. Inside is the main quay pointing northwards, alongside which small coasters and trawlers are usually berthed. The extremities of the mole and quay are lit.

7

Berth. Only very small yachts and motor-boats can berth off the quay. Other yachts should anchor in the roadstead 100 yards off in 4 fathoms on a sandy bottom. Shelter here is good except in fresh S.E. winds when the place is quite impossible.

Facilities are close at hand with some good shops and a restaurant and bar on the quay. Fresh water can be obtained from a pump close to the quay. Fuel at Esso pumps is also here. Fresh water showers and washing facilities at the *Diurno* in the town. Local wine, both white and red, may be bought at a reasonable price at *Diposito dei Vino*. Ice at the fish market or from the factory 1 kilometre outside the village. Elba's airport is close inland.

The shallow sandy bay with a bathing beach runs around the nearby coast, and here is a sailing school and bathing amenities.

Three miles west of Marina di Campo is the Gulf of Barbatoria which provides a pleasant temporary anchorage near a hamlet at its head. Continuing round the steep-to west coast one comes to:

Marciana Marina. A delightful little port with attractive green, mountainous surroundings.

Approach & Berth. Chart 3905. The mole which has recently been extended provides deep water for several yachts to berth inside beyond the old tower. Anchor should be laid out about S.S.E. Good holding and very fair shelter.

Facilities. A water-tap is near the root of the mole. Shops and restaurants a few hundred yards along the road towards the village. The local wine—*Promico del l'Elba*—is excellent. Ice factory behind the village.

Marciana Marina was once the 'country house' district of the island. The village is attractive with its colour-washed houses, tamarisks and oleanders, a setting that had so pleased Napoleon that he ordered the addition of mulberry trees. Ascending the green, mountainous hinterland one reaches Altmarciana, the former mountain retreat for the villagers of the seaport in the event of attack by pirates. Above this village, approached by a track, is the monastery of the Hermitage, where Napoleon accommodated the Countess Walewska during her brief visit to the island. On the mountain slope, too, is the village of Poggia with Fonte Napoleone, where the Emperor drank the waters and where there is now the fashionable Grand Hotel Fonte Napoleone. It was originally planned that Napoleon should make his escape from Marciana Marina, but his naval advisors eventually decided that shelter in the port at that time was too undependable.

A delightful excursion is the drive to Poggio, thence to Altamarina where an aerial railway carries one to the top of Mount Capanne (3,300 feet)—in all taking about three hours.

Island of Pianosa is monotonous, flat and entirely given over to an open prison. Permission to visit the place must first be obtained from the authorities in Elba; but yachts seldom come here. The distinguishing feature when approaching the anchorage from any direction is the islet of La Scala which is higher than the island itself. The bi-weekly steamer puts in at Cala San Giovanni, at the head of which is the village with its white sandy beach.

Pianosa, which has no redeeming feature to break its monotony, has been used for grazing and growing crops, being partially inhabited by a few shepherds and their families. It has always been assumed to be a dependency of Elba. Hence Napoleon, when King of Elba, paid the island an official visit taking with him his personal staff and two horses. He decided to settle a hundred of the former Elban farming families on Pianosa, and to protect them with a garrison of Elban soldiers. On a subsequent visit he saw the establishment of the garrison, but the scheme was never completed.

Island of Gorgona, the most northern of the Tuscan group, is mountainous with a small fishermen's harbour at the foot of a steep-to cove on the E. shore—useful as a night anchorage. The island is an open prison.

Approach, Chart 3901. On entering the harbour give the molehead 20 yards berth on account of underwater ballasting.

Berth. Let go about 30 yards inside the entrance and run out a warp to a bollard on the quay under the cliffs. Sheltered except between E. and N.E. but in emergency one could move for better protection close to the breakwater.

Officials. Military guards.

Facilities. Fruit and fish may be bought. There is a fisherman's bar and a Post Office. The harbour is clean enough for bathing.

Most of the buildings are for the administration of the convicts and for their agricultural training. One is not allowed to land without permission from the military guards.

The island has been occupied by small groups of settlers, off and on throughout the centuries, but never having been properly defended it was, until recent times, a constant prey for pirates. Even repeated attempts by monastic orders to settle on the island have had to be abandoned. For the last hundred years it has been a prison.

Island of Capraia. The small fishing port with its tumbledown village has an interesting approach.

Approach. Chart 158. Sailing Directions should be studied before approaching through the 10-foot channel. The end of the S. mole should be kept in transit with the chapel. The end of the N. mole, which is lit, should be given a wide berth on account of submerged obstructions.

9

Berth. A yacht may lie stern to the quay with the anchor laid out on a sandy bottom. There are depths of about 2½ fathoms inside the harbour shelving towards the quay where there are bollards. The harbour is clean and used only by fishing-craft and a few yachts.

Facilities are few, the place being somewhat primitive with two small hotels and a restaurant. Hydrofoil service plies daily between Porto Ferraio and Piombino.

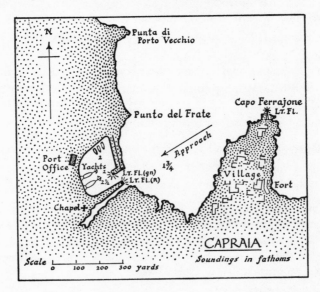

A line of grey houses forms the frontage of the small village; this, together with the dreary prison buildings, makes the aspect depressing. The old fortress of San Giorgio has some 15th-century inscriptions.

During the recent centuries there have been occasions when Capraia has been of interest to the British. On a stormy November day in 1765 Boswell was travelling in a small sailing vessel from Corsica to Genoa when they ran into a northerly gale and were forced to put into Capraia for shelter. The inn having only 'one inconvenient bed', Boswell sought the hospitality of the Franciscan friars whom he found 'hospitable without cunning'. During his seven-day enforced stay Boswell wrote a detailed description of the island. Having no defences at this time Capraia was a constant prey to pirates.

In the Napoleonic Wars it was seized from the Genoese, first by the Corsicans under Paoli, and then by the French. It became a nuisance to British communications with Corsica, which at this time was used by Nelson's ships. Nelson himself, in 1796, led a combined operation to turn out the French, but had no force available to leave behind for Capraia's defence. A few years later the people asked for protection against pirates, but it was still impossible to spare any troops for garrison duties. Nelson, in March 1800, therefore detached *Queen Charlotte*, a ship-of-the-line, from Leghorn to rid Capraia of this menace; but unfortunately when passing Gorgona this fine ship caught fire and was burnt out with the loss of 626 lives.

Island of Montecristo. A small conical island, mountainous, with much cover and a steep-to coast without shelter.

> **Approach and Anchorage.** There are no off-lying dangers, and the only possible anchorage is at Cala Maestra about midway along the western shore. Here one may anchor only in calm weather in the middle of the bay on a sandy bottom in depths of 4 to 5 fathoms; it is best to run a warp ashore to a rock. In a shallow-draught yacht one can anchor closer inshore in very calm weather and run a warp out to the small jetty. The bay, the sides of which are fairly steep-to, is entirely open between N.N.W. and S.W., and sometimes squalls come off the land with winds from other directions. One may normally land in the dinghy at the jetty—a path leads up the valley. See *M. & P.*

Montecristo is inhabited only by a few gamekeepers, who have a shooting-lodge near the landing place. They have no objection to a yacht coming here and are friendly to those wishing to land. The island was stocked with game between the two world wars when, for part of this period, it was the King of Italy's shooting preserve. Today there is little to see: only what remains of a one-time very rich monastery. Many accounts of its history have been handed down, culminating in its being sacked by corsairs; there are stories of its buried treasure, and accounts of treasure-seekers' attempts to find it. No one seems to know precisely how Dumas got his story nor who was the mythical count. In the last century after the ending of piracy, various eccentric individuals went to live there, including an Englishman who is said to have styled himself the Count of Montecristo. With the abdication of the King, the Republic of Italy leased the island to a Milanese family who still retain it.

Island of Giglio. A charming, mountainous little island with a small colourful port, but gradually being overrun by tourists.

The Port

Approach. Chart 3902. A castellated village stands out on the mountain, and around the port can be seen the semi-circle of colour-washed houses and a small red-painted lighthouse at the end of the mole. A yacht should keep within 30 yards of this when turning into the port.

Berth. The harbour is very small. Secure stern to the quay with bows S.E. and anchor in about 2½ fathoms. One should beware of the rocky ledge which protrudes slightly underwater from the quay, and also when letting go the anchor, watch for the heavy chain which runs along the bottom from the W. end of the mole to the steamer quay. At night the port is sometimes floodlit.

Port GIGLIO

Officials. Harbour Master and Customs have an office in the S.E. corner of the port.

Facilities. Fresh water taps are on the quay and at the steamer jetty. A petrol pump is also nearby. Provisions may be bought in the village and a pleasant local dry wine may be bought in the port at Bar Jolly. The ferry-steamer from Sto. Stefano runs daily. The harbour is unsuitable for bathing, but steps at the end of the mole can be used and the water here is usually clean; there is also a sandy beach south of Castellani Point, half an hour's walk. Buses run to Castello morning and evening.

The island's population is only about 2,000, half of whom live in the port, the others mostly occupying the dilapidated Aragonese walled-village (1,500 feet up the mountain), called Castello. In earlier times, from Barbarossa to Napoleon, when the Turks made a number of raids on this island, the whole population would retreat to Castello for refuge. Today the walls and houses are slowly crumbling away, for the inhabitants are gradually moving out to seek employment in the port or on the mainland. Their former rural occupations of growing corn and working in the vineyards have declined, and the island has become rather poor. One can still buy a local white wine (semi-dry) called Ausonica.

Island of Giannutri, the smallest of the Tuscan group, is featureless and undulating. Hitherto its attraction lay in its isolation; one could land, walk across the green maquis which covers the whole island and explore the Roman villa overlooking the sea, without perhaps seeing a soul, unless it were one of the Scaletta family from their summer house at Cala Maestra. The ruins of the sumptuous Roman villa of perhaps twenty centuries ago consists mainly of broken columns some still crowned with their capitals. They form an attractive foreground close above the blue sea; patches of mosaic pavement embellish the scene. Suddenly this tranquillity has begun to change, for the island is condemned to development; scattered villas are springing up indiscriminately and already a couple of villages are planned, one at Spalmatoio (together with a small harbour) and one

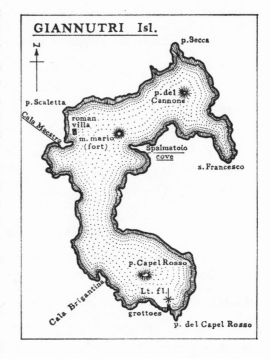

at Cala Maestra. Here a small quay has been built and a mooring buoy laid out to enable freighters to land the building material now much in demand.

Sea communication with Porto Ercole has been established and supplies of water arrive regularly from the mainland.

A comparatively safe place to land is Spalmatoio Cove, but in event of Sirocco weather Cala Maestra on the west coast is more sheltered.

(a) Spalmatoio Cove

Approach. Chart 158. The cove in the N.W. corner of the gulf is easy to find. A small blockhouse on the hilltop bearing about W. leads one into the cove which is only 200 yards long and 100 yards wide. San Francesco Point should be given a wide berth as it protrudes some 30 yards under water.

Berth. Let go in 3 or 4 fathoms and run out a warp to the rocks. There are sandy patches among the rocky slabs, and the shelter is reasonable except from S.E.—a direction unusual in summer. One can land in the dinghy near a fisherman's hut.

(b) Cala Maestra

Approach. A yacht may proceed into the cove without fear of off-lying hazards. The Roman villa may be seen close above.

13

Anchorage. Let go in convenient depths when abreast a concrete pier. The bottom is mostly sand sometimes interspersed with rock. It is advisable to run out a stern warp to the rocks at the head of the cove. One may land in the dinghy at a small quay.

Campese Bay is open, with a long sandy beach, and being used by the ore ships to embark pyrites, it is not agreeable for a yacht.

Approach. Chart 3905. After clearing the two shoals make for Campese Tower.

Anchorage. Let go 50 yards W. of the tower, about 70 yards off the beach in 3 fathoms.

A small hamlet lies in this corner of the bay, and in the S.W. corner are pylons supporting a cable to the ore tip. Close off are holding-off buoys to assist the ore ships.

THE MAINLAND COAST

Opposite the Tuscan Islands on the nearby mainland coast are one or two sheltered coves and some small river-mouth ports. The first port is:

Piombino, the mainland ferry-port for Elba, which is purely commercial.

Approach. Chart 1719 plan shows the place clearly.

Berth temporarily at the Premuda quay near the Port Office and Customs, or more peacefully at the southern quay (*Molo Batterie*). Good shelter but unpleasant surroundings. The Pontile Elba is constantly in use by the Elba ferry-boat. Uncomfortable in a westerly blow.

Facilities. Fresh provisions close by. The town is about a mile inland; taxis available. Piombino Central Station is on the main line. Information kiosk is on the quay with English spoken.

Although no yacht would put in to Piombino for choice, it is worth remembering that Populonia, an old Etruscan town, can be reached by a walk through the cork woods. There is now only a village and a medieval castle here, but the place was once famous, not only for smelting the Elban iron ore, but also the tin and copper from the mines in the vicinity.

The coast then trends for 40 miles in a S.E. direction, the mountains being broken by river deltas. The canal or river ports are of small interest to a yacht.

Forno Cove, S.E. of the Ombrone River is quite deserted, with convenient anchorage and good holding on a flat sandy bottom open between W. and N.W., but a pleasant place in settled weather.

Talamone a well sheltered but very small basin at the entrance to the Orbetello Canal. The walled village lying close behind the port is worth a visit.

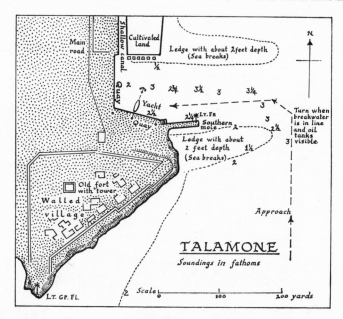

TALAMONE
Soundings in fathoms

Approach. Chart 158. On rounding Cape Uomo keep 2 cables offshore until the silos at the head of the basin bear about west. Then turn to W. passing through the approach channel which has about 3 fathoms depth. The extremities of the extensive ledges on either side are not buoyed and a current often sets into the bay.

Berth. A yacht can lie at the south side of the newly built quay where shelter is good. Bottom is mud, with depths of 2 to $2\frac{1}{2}$ fathoms.

Facilities. Provisions in the village—water at the quay. Bus service to Grosseto and to Rome.

The walled village fortified in the Middle Ages has been completely restored after war damage. The place was named after Telamon, King of Salamis who, on return from the Argonaut expedition, landed here. In more modern times, Garibaldi's expedition put in here in 1860. A small force of irregulars was sent inland to create a diversion, hoping that the Papal States might be deceived as to Garibaldi's real intentions. After topping up with coal the two steamers continued on the voyage conveying 'The Thousand' to the scene of the planned operation—Sicily.

Continuing southward the tall Monte Argentario can be seen rising above the rocky and rather bare peninsula.

Porto Santo Stefano, a pleasant, thriving trawler port with yacht repair facilities and tourist amenities.

Approach and Berth. Chart 1719, plan. A yacht has the choice of two alternatives for berthing:

(a) The town quay, which is cleaner and more airy, is recommended in settled weather. The plan shows the best berths for a yacht.

(b) The harbour, which is the better choice if weather conditions are disturbed.

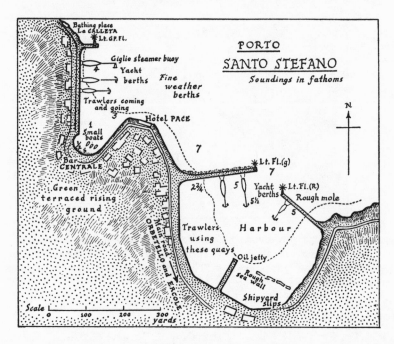

A new mole extending in a N.W. direction from the S.E. shore now affords much better protection within. This mole, however, has no quay and a yacht must run out a long stern warp, the anchor being laid to the S.W. Many yachts berth at the opposite quay if they can find space. The depths here are 3 to 4 fathoms, the bottom being mud. Trawlers are apt to make the port crowded and small tankers sometimes discharge at the inner jetty.

Officials. The Harbour Office is on the quay on the front near the Giglio steamer's summer berth.

Facilities. There are many hotels, shops, restaurants, and bars nearby. Water is laid on at the town quay and at the harbour moles. Many yachts take advantage of the yacht yard (*Cantiere Navale dell'Argentario*) under British direction which undertakes considerable repair work and lays up yachts in winter. A mobile crane lifting 7½ tons is available.

Daily bus service to Rome—3 hours; mainline trains pass through Orbetello—half an hour by bus. The Giglio ferry steamer runs daily from the town quay.

Porto Santo Stefano which extends from the quayside up the slopes of the hill, has 14,000 inhabitants. It has made a complete recovery after being eighty per cent destroyed in the Second World War, and now attracts a number of tourists, and some foreign residents who have built villas at the foot of the mountains above the sea. The main occupation of the port is fishing, the catch being sent daily to Rome by lorry.

In late medieval days Santo Stefano was a small commercial city state with considerable influence on the nearby ports. At the Battle of Lepanto the knights of Santo Stefano provided twelve ships.

Porto Ercole, until very recently a charming little fishing port lying between two hills crowned with Aragonese forts. Rapidly changing with modern building and tourism.

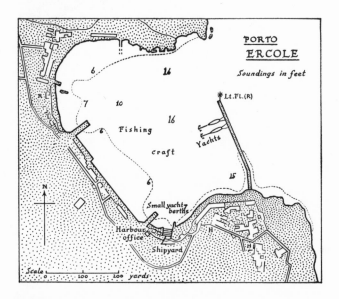

Approach and Berth. Chart 1719, plan. With the building of the breakwater in recent years the harbour is periodically dredged, and the depths are convenient even for large yachts to berth here. The breakwater is of rough stone and has no quay, and the ballasting extends up to 10 yards under water. Yachts therefore berth with anchors to the westward and secure long stern warps to the breakwater. Smaller yachts often find room to berth at the south eastern of the two inner piers where there are 10-foot depths at the pierhead. The bottom generally is sand, mud and small boulders. Shelter here is good. Land by dinghy at one of the inner piers. Fishing craft, which are often active, berth near the shore between the piers. [See photograph facing p. 32.]

From Grotte a breakwater has recently been built extending about 50 yards to the N.E.

Facilities. Fresh provisions are easily obtained, and there are now some good hotels and restaurants on the quayside. Fresh water is piped to both stone piers, and there is a Shell depot near the northern pier.

Officials. The Harbour Office is close by the root of the south-eastern quay.

The port was much damaged in the Second World War, but in recent years there has been considerable reconstruction and the two villages of Porto Ercole and Grotte (on the N.W. corner of the islet) have now joined up and from southward appear as one.

Corsica and Sardinia

A choice of routes

The dark line on the opposite plan shows the route taken by the majority of yachts visiting these islands from the mainland; usually arriving on the N.W. coast of Corsica they cruise southward calling at the ports and inlets on the west coast and at the islands in the Bonifacio Strait; they then follow the Sardinian coast to the end of the newly-developed Costa Smeralda. The ports are therefore described in this order.

The description of the remaining Corsican ports is completed by following the eastern shores from Bonifacio Strait to Cap Corse. In Sardinia the remaining ports are described in a clockwise direction, following the coast from Costa Smeralda round the island and back to the Bonifacio Strait.

In the two islands there are some eighty ports or anchorages of interest to a yacht, the majority of these lying on the dark lined route shown on the map. Very few yachts will be found in other areas; they are mostly those which are able to spend several weeks cruising throughout the summer.

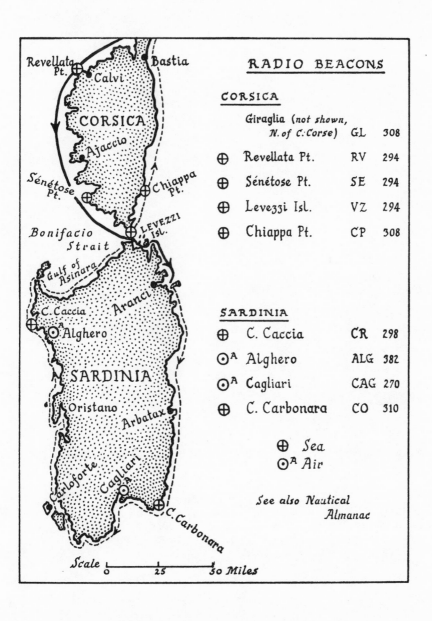

RADIO BEACONS

CORSICA

	Giraglia (*not shown, N. of C.:Corse*)	GL	308
⊕	Revellata Pt.	RV	294
⊕	Sénétose Pt.	SE	294
⊕	Levezzi Isl.	VZ	294
⊕	Chiappa Pt.	CP	308

SARDINIA

⊕	C. Caccia	CR	298
⊙ᴬ	Alghero	ALG	382
⊙ᴬ	Cagliari	CAG	270
⊕	C. Carbonara	CO	310

⊕ Sea
⊙ᴬ Air

See also Nautical Almanac

CORSICA

GIRAGLIA Isl.

CAPRAIA Isl.

Centuri • Macinaggio

CORSE Peninsula

ELBA

Bastia

St. Florent

Ile Rousse

PIANOSA Isl.

Calvi

Galeria

Girolata

Porto

CORSICA

N

Sagone

Ajaccio

Les SANGUINAIRES

P. Pollo

Propriano

Portovecchio

Campo Moro

Tizzano

Sta. Manza

Figari Bay

LAVEZZI Isl.

Bonifacio

Bonifacio Strait

SARDINIA

WEST COAST (N. to S.)
Cap Corse Peninsula
Centuri
St. Florent
Ile Rousse
St. Ambrogio
Calvi
Galeria
Girolata Bay

Porto
Cargese
Port Sagone
Port Provençal
Fico Cove
Ajaccio
Sainte Barbe
Port Cacao
Port Pollo
Propriano
Campo Moro
Port Tizzano
Roccapina
Fornello
Figari Bay

SOUTH COAST
Bonifacio
The Piantarella Channel
Island of Lavezzi
Island of Cavallo

EAST COAST (S. to N.)
Santa Manza
Porto Rondinaro
Porto Nuovo
Porto Santa Giuglia
Portovecchio
Bastia
Port Macinaggio

2

Corsica

*'I had got upon a rock in Corsica, and jumped
into the middle of life'* BOSWELL

About the size of Wales, Corsica is very mountainous with large forests and
steep valleys. As well as the more important sea ports there are large villages in
the mountains, and hamlets sometimes on the mountain-tops; scattered farm-
steads are not to be found.

The west coast is beautiful and the scenery dramatic, providing both a
delightful cruising ground for yachts, and sufficient anchorages suitable in all
weather. The Gulf of Porto is especially remarkable for the contrasting features
of a rugged shore-line with crimson pinnacles of rock against a background of
green forests rising up the mountains behind. On the west these sometimes
reach 9,000 feet and fall away to alluvial plains on the east. The slopes are
largely covered with maquis, an undergrowth of holm-oak, juniper, arbutus
lentisk, buckthorn, heath, bay, myrtle and box; also occasionally found is rose-
mary, lavender and climbing clematis. The name *maquis*, or *macchia*, also gave
its title to the Resistance formations originating in Corsica in the Second World
War. Used in this sense it was the revival of the flame of revolt first kindled
when the local patriots rose against the Genoese more than two centuries ago.

In early historical times, Corsica was occupied by many seafaring traders;
Etruscans and Carthaginians were later followed by Romans, a number of
whom settled in the island. Strabo described the country as affording a poor
livelihood, 'those who occupy the mountains and live from brigandage are
more savage than wild animals': and Seneca, who spent eight years here under
banishment called the people 'robbers, liars, and atheists': but the Sicilian
historian Diodorus Siculus, wrote that 'the islanders live among themselves
with a humanity and justice beyond other barbarians'. In the Middle Ages
came the Pisans, who unlike their predecessors, left behind some architecture,
though nearly all the surviving medieval structures are the churches of the

Romanesque and Baroque periods mostly built by the Genoese who came later. After four centuries of rule the Genoese, being unable to assert themselves any longer, transferred the sovereignty of the islands to France. Apart from brief interludes Corsica has now been two hundred years under French administration.

The state of the population has hardly changed during the past two centuries, and today only a quarter of a million people live on the island. Although nearly half of the land is claimed to be fit for agriculture, it had until recently been very little developed, and only in the last few years have modern methods of irrigation been effectively applied on the east side of the island, where orange groves and vines are starting to be cultivated. Minerals are no longer worked. These earlier unsatisfactory economic conditions gradually caused many of the younger Corsicans to migrate to the French mainland, but the void has to some extent been filled by those repatriated recently from the North African colonies. The island has also improved its finances by the encouragement of tourism.

In the country a century ago, travellers reported seeing deer and mouflon in the forests; but now the few remaining have to be protected. The Romans recorded the presence of monkeys and Boswell claims to have seen sheep, sometimes with six horns. Today there are many boar, foxes and hares, but no rabbits or wolves. Of wild birds there are eagles and vultures, the usual European game birds, and a variety of the smaller species. The forests consist mostly of pines, but there are also oaks and chestnuts. The chestnuts were once used for making a form of bread; in Corsica the timber of this tree grows unusually hard and was used extensively in boat-building.

There is good trout fishing in some of the mountain streams, and one should obtain a permit from the local authority.

Weather. The prevailing summer wind is from the N.W., and during June and July gentle breezes may be expected when, under these conditions, even the more open anchorages may be used. In the southern half of the island the inlets mostly face south of west, a direction which gives better protection from the swell after the day breeze has died away, and also shelter from a Mistral if required. The occasional *Libeccio* from the S.W. is also experienced, and makes these ports unsafe.

The Mistral is the name given to the N.W. wind, sometimes of gale strength, emanating from the Gulf of Lions. Its force may be fully effective in the seas between Corsica and the Balearics although it often does not reach so far south. Coming out of a blue sky from the Rhone valley this gale strikes the waters relatively close to the coast, immediately setting up a rough sea and causing a long swell to spread fanwise across the area between Corsica and the Balearics. Weather forecasts announce the progress of the Mistral and though the swell may be felt acutely off Corsica the gale itself may not appear for a day or more; sometimes it does not reach Corsica at all for it is lifted by the high mountains and at other times it dissolves in the upper air without advancing further along its usual southward path. A yacht, however, should always be prepared to seek shelter in the event of a threatened Mistral, although fortunately in summer these winds of gale strength are a rare occurrence.

Approaching Corsica from the west, one often finds poor visibility off this mountainous coast and hence the prospect of identifying the expected landfall is not encouraging. There are, however, some useful radio beacons to help one. See map on page 21.

Communications

Air. Both from Marseilles and from Nice there are daily flights to Ajaccio, Bastia and Calvi.

Sea. From Marseilles to Ajaccio, and from Marseilles to Bastia there are the mail steamers every two days. From Nice to Ajaccio and from Nice to Calvi there is daily communication in summer by Cie. Generale Transatlantique. The Italian line Tirrenia also runs a daily service from Livorno to Bastia and Port Torres.

Interior services in Corsica consist of air connections between the main towns, a spectacular rail journey over the mountains between Bastia and Ajaccio, and many bus services which mostly follow the picturesque coast.

Food and Wine. Food generally is similar to that in France but somewhat more expensive. Fish is to be preferred rather than meat which is often tough. Local wine is produced in the hinterland of Ajaccio, at Figari and Sartene in the south, and at Cervione and Patrimonio in the north, and at Calenzana in the north-west a rosé *Clos de Bernardi* has been recommended, also a white wine *Paviglia* and a red wine *Capitoro*. Wines bearing the label *Syndicat des Producteurs des Vins d'Origine Corse* are usually good; those from Campo d'Unico and Clos Pozzo di Borgo are available in some of the Ajaccio wine shops. Most of these can also be bought fairly cheaply on draught. Aperitifs are also obtainable; Pastis, Cinzano, Dubonnet, as well as the local and rather sweet Myrte and Cedratine.

Generally the standard of amenities falls beneath that of the mainland. Only in the larger towns, Calvi, Ajaccio and Bastia can one expect better things. Prices are perceptibly more than on the mainland.

Fish. Many underwater fishermen now visit this rocky coast and find the following fish: *rouget* (red mullet), *rascasse* (Med. only, used in *bouillabaisse*), *loup de mer* or *ragnola, denti* (bream), *sardene* (small pilchards), *deurade* or *dorade* (gilthead), *congre* and *murico* (conger and moray eels) which in Roman times were just as great a delicacy as they are today.

Language. Corsican is universally spoken among the Corsicans themselves, in cities and towns as well as the country—though they are courteous enough to speak French to tourists. In country districts there are still many old people who neither speak nor understand French. Corsican is considered to be a dialect, rather than a language, and dates, like the place names and family names, from the three hundred years of Genoese occupation.

Whales off Corsica. The waters north of Cape Corse are unusually deep, and a yacht proceeding towards this cape from approximately the Franco-Italian frontier should not be surprised to see a school of large sperm whales. They are said to be the aging bulls who bring a few cows in from the Atlantic and spend their declining years cruising in these waters.

The first report of one of these whales being captured was in 1620 when it was found to exceed 100 feet in length; there have been many since. These mammals, which are very large, are no longer hunted, and are often to be heard when they surface on a calm night.

Pilotage information—See *Mediterranean Pilot*, Vol. II.

Corsican Heroes: Paoli and Napoleon. The 18th century was a period of national revolt. In 1767 Pasquali Paoli, Corsican patriot, threw off the Genoese yoke and for a short time ruled the island. Corsica, however, came under French sovereignty a couple of years later and owing to internal dissension in the local government Paoli was compelled to flee the island in a British frigate. Earlier friendship with Boswell now helped him to win much sympathy abroad and he was lionised in London. But after nearly twenty years of exile the French Royalists invited him to return to Corsica where in 1790 he was met on arrival by a delegation of representatives. Among them was a young artillery officer, Napoleon Bonaparte, aged twenty-one; they never met again for, after stirring up trouble in Corsica, Napoleon soon fled to France and never returned.

Following threatening measures by the revolutionary government in Paris, Corsica was compelled to seek protection from Britain—an appeal which found favour with the British Cabinet because of the usefulness of Corsican ports. In 1794 Nelson and Hood drove out the French and the island was occupied, but instead of inviting Paoli to govern, Sir Gilbert Elliott was sent out instead.

Corsica was evacuated two and a half years later, but meanwhile Paoli had returned to England where in 1807 he died at the age of eighty-two and, like other Roman Catholics who died in London at this time, was buried in Old St. Pancras cemetery. But in Westminster Abbey a fine memorial bust was erected. Beneath it are inscribed these words: 'To the memory of Pasquali de Paoli, one of the most eminent and most illustrious characters of the age in which he lived. . . .'

Corsica was subsequently handed over to the French at the Treaty of Versailles, soon afterwards becoming a 'department' of France, which it has since remained.

The **Cap Corse Peninsula**—about 25 miles in length, with a central mountain range (4,000 feet)—has a beautiful coastline resembling an unspoilt Riviera. Boswell, writing two hundred years ago, went into some detail, 'The prospect of the mountains', he wrote, 'covered with vines was extremely agreeable and the odour of the myrtle and other aromatic shrubs and other flowers that grow around was very refreshing.'

It is well worth exploring, but only by road, preferably from St. Florent or from Bastia, for there is no suitable port on the peninsula, except perhaps for a small yacht in very settled weather either at Centuri or at Macinaggio on the east side.

Centuri, a picturesque little port for fishing boats; it is only possible for a very small yacht to moor temporarily in the outer port.

> **Approach and Berth.** Chart 1126, plan. This place should be entered in settled weather and clear visibility. A small yacht should not exceed 5 feet draught. Approach is not always easy on account of the surf, and shore objects on the cliff—the square castle, a mill, etc. (see Sailing Directions)—must be identified. The red beacon marking the shoal at the entrance should not be depended upon. The port is sometimes reported to have silted. It is open between W. and N. and subject to an uncomfortable swell. A yacht should *not* anchor off Morsiglia as the bottom is rocky.

> **Facilities.** A water tap, a grocer's shop and a small inn-restaurant.

Centuri was Boswell's port of arrival in Corsica in 1765; he had sailed from Leghorn and having disembarked all his baggage, spent the first night at Morsiglia, a mile up country.

Following the coast southwards for 10 miles one can admire the mountainous scenery as far as the village of Nonza—'stuck in the rudest cliffs like a little nest'. Seven miles further one enters the Gulf of St. Florent.

St. Florent. An exposed and poor anchorage in delightful mountain scenery, by a poor, tumbledown Genoese village.

Approach. Chart 1083. By day all marks are easy to discern including the beacon on Tegnosa Rock.

Anchorage. The most secure, though remote, anchorage is in Fornali Roads. Near the village of St. Florent and about 2 cables from the moles one may anchor S.E. of Tegnosa Rock according to draught. The bottom is partly rocky, the holding uncertain, and the shelter poor. Inside the small basin by the old quays dredging has recently taken place and small yachts can find limited space near the quay with much better shelter.

Facilities. The shops are poor, although in recent years with the development of tourism there has been an improvement. One can eat at each of the three hotels (one is two star). A bus runs to Bastia and another service runs round Cap Corse—a very spectacular tour. The Sailing School and the Underwater Swimming School are well patronised.

This 15th-century village is in a state of disrepair. This is largely explained by the fact that until recent years the marshland at the head of the bay caused so much sickness that people could scarcely live here and the garrison was changed every month. The crumbling Genoese fort guarding the port has witnessed many naval actions in the Gulf. The Mortella Tower, now in ruins, once played an important part in the St. Florent defences. In 1794 when ships of the British fleet, led by Lord Hood, attempted to reduce the town by bombardment they were unable to cripple the tower sufficiently to force its surrender. This was brought about later, but only after a concerted attack with the aid of a strong shore party. The fort's unexpected defiance and ability to resist made an impression on defence experts generally, and called for visits by engineers who made detailed drawings. A few years later, when Napoleon caused an invasion scare in England, a line of fortified towers, similar to that at Mortella, were built on the Kent and Sussex shores; but the name had become corrupted, and these became known as Martello towers. The French have not forgotten this remarkable action, and one hundred and forty years later when Admiral Lord Cunningham visited St. Florent in H.M.S. *Hood*, the mayor presented him with a lithograph showing Lord Hood's ships attacking this famous tower.

Known as San Fiorenzo until recent years, the anchorage, although so inferior with its poor holding and uncomfortable swell, has been used by warships in every campaign. Despite the conditions the loss of only one British warship has been recorded. This was in 1795 when the sloop *Fleche*, fourteen guns, ran on the reef off Fornali Tower and although the ship was lost, the whole crew was saved.

Ile Rousse. A fairly well-sheltered port in summer, connected by road—1 mile—to a recently modernized village with new hotels and restaurants.

Approach. Chart 1126 and plan.

Berth. Secure stern to inner end of the mole with bows S.W. and anchor in 4 fathoms. If no steamer is expected one can lie temporarily alongside, or there is sometimes room to anchor off. In the event of winds between N. and E. one must clear out.

Facilities. There is nothing to be got in the port, and one must walk to the village, where there are shops, a restaurant and an engineering workshop. The large Hotel Napoleon, which for many decades made the place fashionable, was closed in 1968 and has been superseded by half a dozen smaller hotels. One or two good restaurants have also sprung up in recent years. A sandy beach extends round the bay. The summer passenger service from Nice to Ile Rousse was diverted in 1968 to Calvi instead.

The village of old houses has more than 2,000 inhabitants, but is of no particular interest except for the shopping at the small San Paoli Square. This is shaded by palm trees with a fruit market on one side, and in the centre is a white marble bust of the hero of Corsica. It was Paoli who founded the port in order to take the place of Calvi, at that time held by the Genoese. He used it as a base for raids on Genoese shipping and for communicating by boat with Nelson's ships and although the port later became useful for exporting oranges and local fruit, it now serves little practical purpose, except in summer for a few tourists.

When landing from the yacht to buy provisions it is recommended to take the dinghy across to the beach in order to shorten the return walk when heavily laden. On the north side of the port are some attractive bathing beaches of fine sand.

Before reaching Calvi, one should put in at a small yacht port on the western side of Algaiola Bay. This is **St. Ambrogio** lying at the foot of a recently developed villa estate.

Approach and Berth. Plan on Chart 1126. This small port is tucked in at the head of a cove facing N.E. A short mole extending from shore on a S.E. direction provides good shelter; its extremity is lit at night. A yacht should steer for the molehead on a S.W. course and when inside berth at one of the quays in depths of about 2 fathoms.

This place is being developed and a number of villas have recently been built.

Calvi, an attractive, sheltered port in beautiful mountainous surroundings.

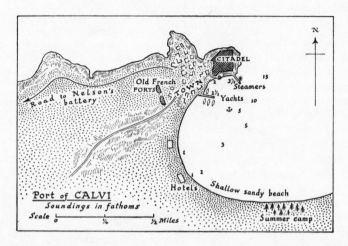

Approach. Chart 1126. The citadel stands out at a distance. After rounding the end of the breakwater, a yacht should proceed either to the anchorage or the quay.

Anchorage. A yacht has the choice of either (a) anchoring, or (b) berthing at a new quay extending for 75 yards in a direction 324° from Cape de l'Orient. [Photograph facing p. 33.]

(a) There is plenty of room to anchor in a good lee under the breakwater and citadel of Calvi, though room must be left for the steamer to turn and berth alongside. In a Mistral the anchorage is well sheltered; but in the more shallow depths the holding is not good.

(b) At the new quay there are depths of 2 fathoms at its extremity and 1½ fathoms near the root. Bow moorings with conical buoys are laid on either side of the quay thus enabling a yacht to berth stern-to. A small charge is made.

Facilities. A water hydrant is available close to the Round Tower on the commercial quay and at the new quay are water connections spaced at intervals. An early morning market opens for fresh provisions and there are shops; but prices are not cheap. Diesel fuel is available in any quantity and can be delivered at the quay. Ice can be bought from a factory on the waterfront, and here are also some restaurants. There are at least six hotels in the town, three of them being most modern; and outside the town are others, together with a Youth Camp. There is a civil airfield, and both bus and rail communication with the other towns.

Calvi, a town of only 3,000 people, rises on a peninsula to a commanding position almost surrounded by sea. The old Genoese citadel, still enclosed by ramparts, some dating from the 13th century, stands on its highest point. The

Porto Ercole

The approach to Porto Azzuro, Elba

The Citadel at Calvi, Corsica

Bonifacio, the rocky south coast of Corsica

Corsican mountain ranges following the contours of the bay, form the background to a turquoise sea, with a long, sandy beach and pine-wooded foothills. The setting could not be more lovely. Fortunately modern development has come slowly and the old streets, small shops, bars and old-fashioned hotels inside the town are very little changed in recent years.

From the town one should climb up to the top of the fortifications for the magnificent view. On the way one passes by a square with a 17th-century barracks, formerly the old Palace of the Governors; a Baroque church is close by.

About 2 kilometres outside the town and set on a large granite rock is a small defaced tablet inscribed: *Ici Nelson dirigeant le feu des batteries contre Calvi perdit un œil 12 Juillet 1794.* His Hill Battery—consisting of two 26-pounders and a 12-inch mortar—was sited on a small plateau high upon the rough mountain slopes, the guns having been landed at an exposed rocky cove at Agro, $3\frac{1}{2}$ miles S.W. from the town of Calvi. Nelson had arrived with H.M.S. *Agamemnon* in company with two frigates and sixteen transports on 17th June, anchoring in a depth of 53 fathoms on a rocky bottom 1 mile from the shore. Together with British troops and Corsican patriots, Nelson had planned to land forty guns from the ships to reduce the Calvi defences; but the day-breeze with an uncomfortable swell, made landing operations very difficult. Once ashore, each 24-pounder required two hundred men to prepare its roadway and drag it the $2\frac{1}{2}$ miles from the landing place to Madona on the limestone heights above. In his report to Lord Hood, Nelson asked that footwear might be sent for the bare-footed sailors. 'The first $\frac{3}{4}$ mile was up a steep mountain, and the other part was not very easy', he wrote. 'The climate here from July to October is most unfavourable for military operations' was another observation only too true, for in *Agamemnon*'s log are noted a number of recordings of winds as being 'strong', 'heavy sea', 'thunder and lighting'; once *Agamemnon* put to sea because of the dangerous weather, and another time the heavy cable parted and the best bower anchor was lost. In August the French garrison surrendered and were given full honours, many being carried in Nelson's ships as free men to Toulon.

A few miles westward of the town are some old churches: St. Rainier at the foot of Mt. Maggiore, La Trinité at Aregno, and St. Pierre at Lumio.

The coast southward of Calvi is the most dramatic and picturesque of the whole island. It is best visited during the settled weather of June and July when gentle westerly sea-breezes usually prevail. In the event of a deterioration in the weather one should make for the nearest safe port—either Calvi or Ajaccio.

The first anchorage sometimes visited by yachts is in the Gulf of Galeria.

Galeria. An open anchorage with a few uninteresting dwellings close by the shore.

Approach and Anchorage. Chart 1126. The ruin of Galeria Tower is easy to discern and one may anchor about 2 cables S.W. of it in 5 fathoms on a clean sandy bottom. It is very exposed. Only a few fishing boats use this place and haul up on the beach, north of the hamlet, which is of recent construction.

Facilities. An excellent fishermen's restaurant on the seashore specializing in langouste.

Rounding the red rocky headlands of Gargalo Island and Pt. Rossa one comes to the Girolata Gulf, the N.E. shores of which conveniently face S.W. and thus afford protection from the occasional Mistral. Leaving the Gulf of Galeria one must round **Gargalo Island,** lying at the S.W. extremity of the gulf, close off the mainland of Corsica.

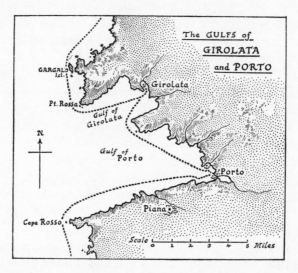

Some of the French guide-books imply that there is plenty of water in the passage between the island and the shore, but English yachts which have attempted to pass through have strongly advised against it. Instead of there being depths of 6 metres as claimed in one guide-book, barely 8 feet have been reported over the rocks in the middle. A realistic description given in Sailing Directions of one hundred years ago reads—'a width of only the length of a brigantine through which small vessels could pass—and a depth of water sufficient for galleys'.

Girolata Bay. A favourite summer anchorage in delightful unspoilt mountain scenery and suitable for a dozen yachts to moor during settled weather.

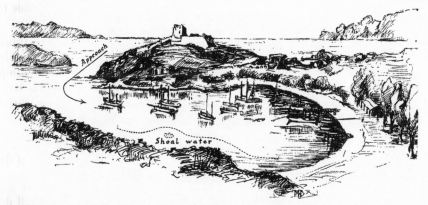

Approach. See Chart 430. Leave Girolata fortress to port and continue into the cove until sounding 6 fathoms. Here the sand gives way to rock and weed, though close under the N.W. shore, patches of sand continue shorewards as the depth decreases. The nature of the bottom can usually be followed in the clear water.

Anchorage. In the N.W. corner of the bay, round the corner behind the castle, there is much more water than charted. There are sheltered berths there for 10 or 12 yachts moored fore and aft, head seawards. The French chart is inaccurate as regards depths which are very irregular; more than 2 fathoms can be found well inside the bay. A S.W. wind brings an uncomfortable swell into the harbour, and yachts are advised to clear out when southerly weather is predicted. There is excellent shelter at a small cove close northward in Elbo Bay.

Girolata inlet, with good bathing in the sandy coves nearby, has two small summer restaurants. Limited provisions can be obtained from one of them; but, if wishing to dine here, one should order in advance, for with only one delivery by sea daily, catering is a difficult problem.

There is always speculation as to the number of yachts that can be safely accommodated in this small harbour. It is, however, interesting to record that in 1545 when John Doria captured the notorious pirate Dragut the latter's whole fleet of eighteen ships was then sheltering in this port.

Continuing into the Gulf of Porto the scenery is considered to be the most spectacular of all—red cliffs, and foothills with green valleys ascending the tall mountains standing close behind. Unfortunately, there is no shelter or suitable anchorage in this large gulf and, if wishing to land at **Porto**, one can only anchor off the beach where a swell invariably rolls in. The police have recently discouraged yachts from doing this.

Approach and Anchorage. Steer for the Genoese tower on the promontory; then anchor close by in 5 fathoms depth off the bathing beach. It is sometimes possible to berth alongside the quay for a short while, but this requires great caution as the 'port' is a mere cut in the rock, and a yacht is not advised to berth here even when conditions are perfect.

35

Facilities. One can land by dinghy on the open beach near some small restaurants and modest hotels. There is nothing much to be bought unless one walks up the hillside to Porto village. Many campers come here in the summer months.

Beyond Cape Rosso (on the S.W. extremity of the gulf), and before reaching the Ajaccio Gulf, are a number of deserted bays with suitable anchorage, mostly facing S.W., thus gaining some protection from the tall headlands shielding them from W. to N.W. wind. Among these bays may be chosen: Cargese Bay, Sagone Bay, Port Provençal, Fico Cove. Some of these are worth a brief description:

Cargese. An open anchorage at the foot of Cargese village.

Approach. From southward the village is easy to discern standing on the shoulder of the hill. Below it a shallow boat harbour has recently been built.

Anchorage. There is no suitable anchorage close by, as the bottom consists of rock and boulders, as well as being very irregular. The boat harbour has 8 feet depths only off the molehead, after which it quickly shelves to 5 feet. The best anchorage is towards the sandy beach at the head of the bay ($\frac{1}{2}$ mile eastward)—smooth, clean sand in 2 to 3 fathoms depths, 100 yards off; but being exposed between S. and W.S.W. it is suitable only in settled weather.

Facilities. The village, lying on the hill, is nearly half an hour's walk from the beach. Fresh provisions may be bought at the shops. There is a café and a new hotel, which benefit from the coach tours bringing tourists from Ajaccio to make lengthy stops at Cargese village. A French Youth Camp is situated round the fringe of the sandy bay.

Although the view over the seaward slopes is impressive, the place has little charm or interest, except for the two churches, Greek Orthodox and Roman Catholic, standing opposite one another. The village was built by the French at the end of the 18th century to house some refugees from Greece who, a hundred years before, had fled from the Turks. To help them in their plight when the Mani was overrun, the Genoese offered sanctuary in Corsica; but it was not until the French built this village that these former fugitives could be satisfactorily accommodated. The full story is given by Patrick Leigh Fermor in his book *Mani**.

Sagone is a deserted, broad, sandy bay (open to S.S.W.) lying in attractive mountain scenery.

Approach and Anchorage. Chart 430. A yacht should approach towards the tower where a short mole with a quay can be seen extending eastwards. The small harbour provides shelter for two or three yachts which can berth on the N. side with anchor laid out north-wards and stern secured to the quay; but this, however, is often crowded with local boats. Depths near the extremity of the quay are about 3 fathoms, decreasing towards the root. A yacht can also anchor off in depths of about 4 fathoms on a bottom of sand with fine weed.

*John Murray, 1958.

Facilities. Three small hotels and two cafés have recently grown up in the vicinity and tourism appears to be encroaching. A bathing beach, steep-to, and of coarse sand, lies at the head of the bay.

The presence of a Genoese tower is frequently a sign that a former trading anchorage lies in the near vicinity. Sagone Tower, still somewhat crumbling, is attractively portrayed in a set of coloured lithographs of a naval engagement hanging on the walls of the United Service Club in London. These prints illustrate phases of a frigate action between the French and British, which took place in the bay close under this tower in May 1812. As a result the tower was damaged by explosions in two of the French vessels which blew up and scattered their burning timber upon it. The French had been attacked by the British frigates, *Pomone*, *Unite* and *Scout*, which, arriving during a calm early in the day, had sighted the French force at anchor close under the tower. Unable to approach further inshore for lack of wind, they hoisted out their boats and were towed into 'grape-shot range' when, after a two-hour hot engagement the French ships, which were partially laden with timber, blew up.

Port Provençal, a small deserted cove, with a sandy beach, lying at the head of Lava Bay in attractive surroundings.

Approach. Chart 430. The two islets on the southern shore are useful marks in helping one to avoid the underwater rocks. The contours of the bay and depths off the beach are similar to those of Fico Cove, see page 38.

Anchorage. One can anchor close off the beach in 2 fathoms, and if desirable, run a warp to the shore. Shelter from the prevailing wind is good.

The place is quite unspoilt, there being only a fisherman's hut and a couple of small houses, but no track leading inland.

The Gulfs of Ajaccio and Valinco have a number of pleasant ports and anchorages in a mountainous setting.

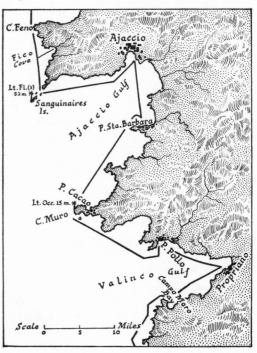

If overtaken by bad weather on this stretch of coast it is well to bear in mind that Ajaccio is a safe port to make for. If southward bound Campo Moro Bay is the nearest safe anchorage, and after this Bonifacio.

Fico Cove is small and deserted, with a sandy beach open between south and west—a temporary, fine-weather anchorage.

Approach. Chart 430. From La Botta rock one may head for the beach, but beware of a 1-fathom patch N. of approach course and the underwater reef from the S. shore close by the anchorage. (This extends nearly 80 yards in a N.W. direction from the visible rocky point.)

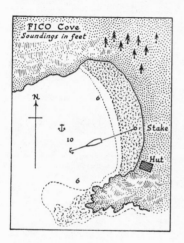

Anchorage. Let go in the centre of the bay, 100 yards from the beach, in 3 fathoms depth on a firm sandy bottom. Although open between S. and W. the configuration of the cove tends to break any swell from N. or W. One can anchor closer in and run a warp ashore.

The place is completely deserted, and the cove is used only by local fishermen as a temporary anchorage. A track leading up the valley enables a few campers to come here in summer. The bathing beach, which is crescent shaped, is about 100 yards long and rather steep-to with 6-feet depths only 15 yards off.

Les Sanguinaires is a reef of red-tinted rocks extending $1\frac{3}{4}$ miles S.W. of Pointe Parate. The pass between the northern islet and Pointe Parate is easy to negotiate in fine weather, being more than 500 yards wide and at least 2 fathoms deep. One should recognize the rock off Pointe Parate and then pass about one-third the width of the channel from this point, where the depths are about 4 fathoms.

Ajaccio the capital of Corsica, a well-protected all-weather port, with all the amenities of a pleasant city close at hand.

Approach. Chart 1126, plan. The towers in the approach are now painted red.

Berth. See sketch plan. Yachts berth with sterns to the quay on the outer breakwater, and also off Quay Napoleon. Recently this quay was widened by encroaching on the harbour basin and the Jetée de la Citadelle was about to be extended. Smaller yachts berth at the inner mole. The harbour becomes very crowded and yacht's anchors are continually fouling one another. The shelter in the port is excellent, but the holding is poor.

Officials. Harbour Master and Customs, whose offices are opposite the steamer berths. A British Consulate in the town.

Facilities. Fresh water is available at both quays, but it is often not drinkable. Both petrol and diesel fuel can be supplied daily from pumps at the angle of the Jetée de la Citadelle. An engineer and a joiner have workshops on the quay. A good morning market opens daily close to Quay Napoleon. A small yacht club at the root of the mole can provide showers; a daily weather report can also be seen at the club. There are many good and not too expensive restaurants nearby, and a number of hotels.

The airport has frequent services to France and England. Steamers go to Nice and Marseilles. Rail terminus for Bastia—a beautiful mountainous journey of five and a half hours. Bathing off the breakwater.

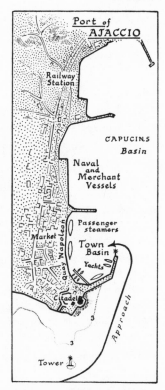

Ajaccio, a city of 42,000 inhabitants, has the atmosphere of a provincial capital. The avenue, gardens, large open-air cafés, some luxurious hotels among the palm trees, and large houses, apart from a few huge modern blocks, are typically 'French Riviera' of the last century. Near the port is the old quarter of the town with its crowded Genoese houses—one of them, Napoleon's birthplace, in a narrow street, is now a museum. This has recently been enriched by a unique collection of family documents and mementos, and was opened in 1967 by Prince Buonaparte.

Although it is sometimes disagreeably hot in summer, Ajaccio has a delightful spring and winter climate, which in the last century was much appreciated by English visitors. They stayed in comfortable hotels with charming views across the calm waters of the Gulf.

In the port, during the summer months, two, and sometimes three, steamers may arrive during the day, bringing from Marseilles and Nice some of the poorer French tourists who soon disappear, making their way to the many summer camps. There are many sightseeing tours which operate on a big scale from Ajaccio. The harbour can be very crowded with yachts. As a result of increased tourism the city appears to be prospering and many modern blocks are growing up on the side of the hill above the residential quarter.

Gulf of Ajaccio—S.E. Shore. There are two night anchorages both of which are pleasant in settled weather:

(a) **Sainte Barbe** lies in a cove formed by a rocky islet and, provided the yacht can get into less than 2-fathom depths, shelter is good; if a swell should come up most of it is broken on the rocks. The shore is sprinkled with summer villas and the surroundings are well planted with colourful shrubs.

(b) **Port Cacao** is a small sandy cove under the cliffs close to Guardiola Point. There are 3-fathom depths on a sandy bottom, but the anchorage is rather exposed to N. A few fishing craft work here with their lobster-pots in summer, otherwise there is no communication.

Port Pollo. A sandy bay with a few houses—not worth a special visit unless one is interested in the neolithic caves only a few kilometres inland.

Approach. Chart 1126, plan. The rock awash S.E. of the 9-foot rock cannot be seen in calm weather and should therefore be given a wide berth. The ruined tower on the hill cannot now be seen from seaward.

Anchorage. Best shelter is usually in the N.W. corner of the bay. There is 3 fathoms depth on patches of sand, but much of the seabed consists of weed on very hard sand and stone.

Facilities. In the small hamlet, which caters for a few summer visitors, there is a hotel-restaurant at the S.W. end of the beach. One can buy some provisions, and there are one or two small bars. The beach in the N.W. corner, though used by bathers, is unsuitable, having weed and boulders close inshore. Many campers come here.

Two conspicuous graves by the ruins of a small castle are without interest, but inland, up the Taravo Valley, are the menhir statues of Filitosa. Dating from about 3,500 B.C. these great burial monuments have only recently been discovered, and are unique among the prehistoric remains now being un-covered in south-west Corsica. They are associated with the same form of early settlements to be seen in Malta, Sardinia and the Balearics, and yet are quite different from the Nuraghi Bronze Age culture of Sardinia.

Propriano. An attractive little port affording fairly good shelter by a small town in a mountainous setting.

Approach. Chart 429. The lighthouse on the molehead is conspicuous, and also a prominent cemetery standing on the E. side of a hill beyond the town. The lighthouse should not be passed too closely as the reef on which it is built extends a few yards under water.

Anchorage. One may anchor as indicated in the plan, and then haul in the yacht's stern to the quay. Alternatively, if no steamers are berthed, one may take advantage of the better shelter inside and secure the stern to the southern end of the steamer quay. Winds between W. and N. cause a swell, and in this event it is best to proceed to P. Pollo.

Officials. Customs and Harbour Master.

Facilities. Good fresh water is usually obtainable by hydrant at the steamer quay, and there is a water-pump in the street by the fishermen's quay. Fresh provisions and stores are available at local shops. Some of the older hotels are in the town, but modern ones, each with their bathing beach, have grown up outside. Restaurants are by the waterfront. Bus communication with Ajaccio and Bonifacio.

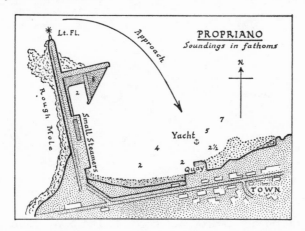

Until recent years the 2,000 inhabitants of Propriano derived a living from the timber trade and from fishing. With the development of tourism they have become prosperous, reflecting a 'new look' in the upkeep of buildings, shops and modern hotels.

Campo Moro. A very pleasant anchorage in a sheltered bay, open only partially to north. Campo Moro is the best anchorage in the Valinco Gulf.

Approach. Chart 1126, plan. Sailing Directions describes the hazards; but the rocks are easily discerned by the gentle surf breaking in.

Anchorage. The S.W. corner of the bay affords the best shelter, but one must sometimes avoid the moorings of fishing vessels laid in depths of about 4 fathoms. Sandy patches with good holding can be found in depths of 5 fathoms. Shelter is good because the offlying rocks break the sea and the swell; only in the northern sector is it slightly open. Even in winter local boats remain here at their moorings.

Facilities. Among the half dozen small houses at each side of the bay is a Post Office and a small general store selling eggs and sometimes bread, but already developers are at work and villas are springing up. A small restaurant has recently opened at the E. end of the beach; if one orders in advance, an appetising meal can be obtained, including lobster. There is a turreted house in the centre of the bay and a good bathing beach lines the shore.

The old Genoese tower is worth a visit for the view. A road now connects Campo Moro with Propriano.

Sailing southward, after 5 miles one reaches the tall, massive promontory of Sénétosa with its two white light towers standing above a white building.

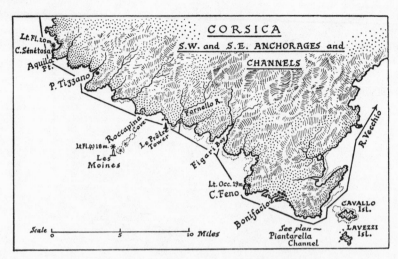

Here is also the Radio Beacon, see page 21. The S.W. point on this massif (Aquila Point) is low, and both this and the headlands already passed have off-lying rocks, and the coast should be given a berth of half a mile.

Three miles further is Tizzano Cove and one must then decide whether to pass inside or outside the rocky shoals of Les Moines. (Les Moines Tower stands 87 feet high and has an 18-mile light.) One should pass outside in bad weather and also by night—the coastal lights are excellent. One may pass inside in fine weather especially when wishing to visit Roccapina and Fornello, described later.

Port Tizzano. A delightful little fishing hamlet lying at the mouth of a river, affording good shelter except from W.S.W.

Approach. Chart 429. If coming from the N., steer for the centre of the peninsula between Latoniccia Point and Avena Bay. The old fort which marks the northern entrance to the inlet may soon be recognised, and then the three or four buildings on the southern shore of the 'port'. When on the line between Cap de Zivia and the village (about 023°) steer for the centre of the inlet, keeping slightly more northward as you get nearer the fort.

Anchorage. With the fort bearing about W.N.W. let go the anchor in a depth of 4 to 5 fathoms; you should then be about one third the distance across from the N. shore. There are patches of sand with good holding.

Facilities. There is nothing to be bought at the fishermen's houses, but ½ mile along the road is a simple restaurant run by one of the fishermen. Lobsters can usually be bought quite cheaply.

An improved road now leads to the important inland village of Sartene. On the opposite side close under the old fort is a small bathing place.

The land around this delightful little inlet has recently been marked out for building sites, and already summer villas are springing up. Higher up the valley some early tombs have recently been excavated.

Roccapina. This cove although well sheltered from all winds in the westerly quarter is so hemmed in by rocks that one would recommend only a shallow-draught yacht or motor-boat to come here.

Approach. Chart 429. The tower on the S.W. headland stands out, and to the N.E. is a remarkable rock resembling a crouching lion. This side of the shore can be followed very closely in minimum depths of about 2 fathoms with rocky outcrops close to the S.E., or alternatively, one can approach from the south side towards the middle of the bay taking care to avoid an underwater rock, lying between two rocky islets, easily seen on a bright day.

Berth. There is anchorage towards the head of the cove in 2 to 3 fathoms on a sandy bottom with room to swing, but this is untenable in southerly winds.

Facilities. Limited fresh provisions from the café a mile inland on top of the hill. Fresh water is sometimes available at a spring the N.W. side at the head of the cove. A minor road leads up the hill eventually joining the Ajaccio–Bonifacio road.

Close under the Genoese tower are the remains of a medieval village. Except for some bathing parties coming by road, the place is deserted and the setting charming.

Fornello. This cove, similar to a number of others on this stretch of coast, affords shelter from the west.

Approach. Chart 429. Both the small Prêtre Beacon (red and black bands) on the rock and the large and prominent Olmeto tower help one to find the entrance. A shoal on the E. side of the centre line of approach must be avoided.

Anchorage. Let go as convenient in 2 to 3 fathoms.

Figari Bay, one of the few river inlets in Corsica, lies in mountainous country and is visited only by fishermen and summer campers. Reasonable shelter but care is required to ensure a safe berth.

Approach. See Sailing Directions and Chart 429. The distant leading mark of Chapelle Sainte cannot be seen during the approach, nor the ruins of Sta. Barbara church shown on Chart 429. Sailing Directions' description is otherwise good.

Anchorage. The holding off the N.E. end of the inlet is poor owing to the thick growth of weed on the bottom. This anchorage, which is the last in the estuary with room to swing, is just S.E. of the little hut on the rock on the north shore. The steep-to sides of the creek and the thick weed on the bottom cause yachts to drag in a Mistral, and even with two anchors out it could not be regarded as safe. French yachts with local knowledge often continue to the head of the estuary, keeping to the middle of the fairway, turning to starboard behind the island and to the N.E. of it. There is no room to swing here, and it is necessary to secure the bows to the shore, but the anchorage offers absolute protection.

The country is mostly scrub and maquis; no dwellings are near the anchorage, only a number of campers in the summer months. Up the valley a number of menhirs have recently been discovered, and beyond the village, near Montilati, is the small, vaulted chapel of St. Quilico.

Bonifacio, a steep-to landlocked harbour overshadowed by an impressive medieval fortress-village.

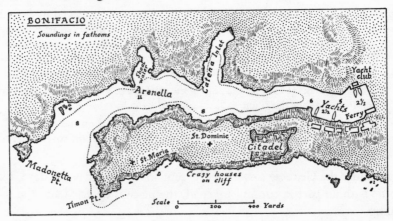

Approach. Charts 1126, plan, and Sailing Directions. If approaching from the west the summits on the Trinité range are very distinctive, and when closer to the coast the houses on the cliff indicate the entrance, which can be easily missed. [Photograph facing p. 33.]

Berth. Yachts proceed to the inner end of the inlet and may berth off the village quay or take advantage of the buoys provided by the Yacht Club (1967) and haul the stern in to their quay. The inner harbour has recently been dredged to 2½ fathoms.

Officials. Harbour Master and Customs with whom the club conveniently deals. Club Bonifacio, formed in July 1967, occupies the old naval building at the N.E. end of the inlet.

Facilities. Water, hot showers, ice and drinks can be obtained at the Club, which is run as a business concern and is expensive. It is hoped shortly to establish laying-up facilities, with labour for repair work; also a Perkins engine repair-shop. It is intended to build a Patent slip in Catena Inlet. Fuel is obtainable at a garage close by or at pumps on the S. side.

Fruit, groceries etc. can be bought at the shops also at the waterside where there are a few restaurants and one of the new hotels. The ferry-steamer to La Maddalena and Sta. Teresa runs twice daily and there is a bus to Ajaccio (4 hours) also twice daily.

On entering this narrow inlet the massive steep-to walls of the fortress are most impressive. Sometimes a garrison is accommodated here, and then one may not enter the military area of the citadel, although one may go inside to visit the two old churches; the 13th-century St. Dominic, built by the Knights Templar, is the only Gothic church on the island. Sante Marie Majeure, built by the Pisans and then rebuilt in the 13th century by the Genoese, is remarkable for the water cisterns which were designed to enable the defenders to withstand a long siege. The walk round the citadel and along the heights above the fort is fascinating and the view of the dilapidated houses standing crazily on the overhanging cliffs on the seaward side of the town, should not be missed. Altogether about two thousand people live in Bonifacio within the citadel where the main shopping centre is also to be found. Until recent years, the presence of the garrison and the regular steamer service, gave the town a livelihood; but much depends now upon tourism and the improved facilities for yachts.

In the 18th century, coral from the adjoining coast was remarkable for the length and firmness of its branches, as well as for the brightness of its colour, which was deep red.

BONIFACIO ~ The entrance from Arenella looking to seaward

ALTERNATIVE ROUTES

After leaving Bonifacio one must decide whether to continue towards the east and round the shores of Corsica, or make for the Maddalena Islands and the anchorages on the northern shores of Sardinia. (*See Chapter 3—Bonifacio Strait.*) Alternative routes are shown and described on pages 20 and 21.

If rounding the southern shores of Corsica, a yacht should make towards the Prêtre Rock beacon (easily distinguished) and then enter the **Piantarella Channel,** fully described in Sailing Directions (Vol. II). This channel can be recommended only by day and in clear weather without an east wind. The two beacons forming the leading marks for the channel are difficult to distinguish, and one must follow the instructions carefully.

The two uninhabited off-lying islands of **Lavezzi** and **Cavallo**, with many outcrops of rocks, are of interest for their rugged charm.

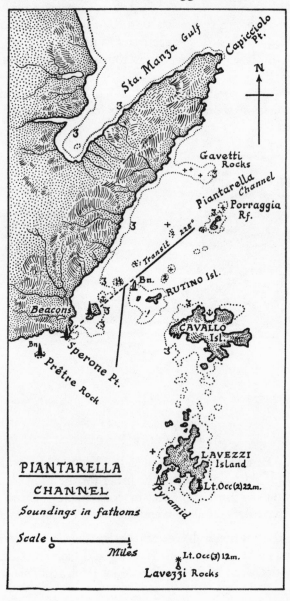

PIANTARELLA

CHANNEL

Soundings in fathoms

Scale

Miles

Many small French yachts make their way here every summer and get to know by experience most of the small sandy coves. The newcomer, however, must study the chart very carefully beforehand and choose suitably calm weather. Were it not for the very clear water one could not detect the more important submerged rocks. For those who enjoy solitude, rock-dodging among the rugged surroundings of these islands can be interesting, but only in a very small yacht or motor-boat.

Island of Lavezzi. There are two small anchorages in this completely barren island, both suitable for a yacht of not more than 20 tons.

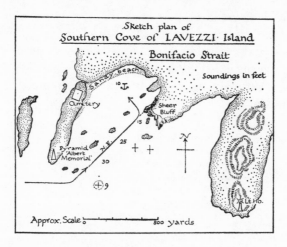

Sketch plan of
Southern Cove of LAVEZZI Island

(a) **Southern Cove**

Approach and Berth. Chart 1189. Though the approach at first sight appears alarming, the following instructions, aided by the sketch plan, should facilitate the entry under power. Make for position south of pyramid on S.W. corner of islet. Pass 15 yards off some small rocks E.S.E. of pyramid and head in a N.E. direction for 500 yards towards a steep bluff, leaving a line of rocks close to port. (The last rock to port is sometimes marked by a white stick.) One can then see two sandy coves, of which the westerly one is the more attractive. Now turn to port, passing between two small outcrops of rock, and following the sandy bottom towards the beach, let go in 10 feet. There is shelter all round, though between S.E. and S.W., the only protection is the clusters of rock.

This is an ideal place, especially in easterly winds, to spend a day bathing, and in settled weather as a night anchorage; but more than one yacht has experienced a sensation of eeriness suggesting that the island is haunted. Close by the beach is a cemetery with a memorial stone recording the loss of the

French frigate *Semillant* in February 1855 when bound for the Crimea. All three hundred and fifty men and four hundred passengers were lost when she foundered off the Lavezzi shoal.

(b) **Greco Cove**—a narrow inlet on the N.E. side of the island suitable in westerly weather.

> **Approach and Berth.** Keep close to the rocky shore steering a westerly course and passing inside a rock awash lying 100 yards offshore. As the cove opens, proceed towards the sandy beach at its head and anchor in 2 fathoms.

Another cemetery of *Semillant*'s victims lies behind the beach.

Island of Cavallo. In calm weather small yachts have the choice of three or four anchorages on this largely barren island. Each is fringed with rocks; submerged, awash and above water, and most of these are accurately shown on Chart 1189. In clear unruffled water with favourable light they can be spotted; but to clarify the principal dangers and suggest a safe approach course a sketch plan has been drawn.

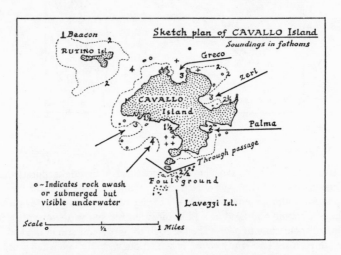

Suggested approaches to coves are shown by the arrows,
to be used in conjunction with Chart 1189.

(a) **Greco Cove**, facing N., should be approached with the eastern headland about 255°. The two rocks shown on the chart as drying 1 and 2 feet respectively are, in fact, just submerged today.

(b) **Zeri Cove.** One should enter on a S.W. course.

Cala Gonone, Sardinia

The entrance to Porto Alghero, Sardinia

The coast of the Messina Strait from Taormina

(c) **Palma Cove.** One should approach by hugging the northern shore, at the same time watching for a submerged rock 100 yards to the southward. There are a number of summer huts above the shores of this cove.

To cross from the east side of the island to the west one may pass in sufficiently deep water by keeping close to the large rocky outcrop shown on the chart.

(d) **The two coves on the S.W. of Cavallo** can be approached more easily. A number of French people have built summer huts close to the beaches.

The granite on this island was quarried by the Romans, and one or two blocks are still awaiting shipment. Some crude bas reliefs on the living rock can also be seen.

Following the Corsican coast northwards one comes to some interesting bays and coves before reaching the large Gulf of Portovecchio.

Santa Manza. A spacious gulf with a long bathing beach at its head. Except in N.E. winds this is the best anchorage—sand. The S.E. shore of the gulf has one or two attractive coves, with sandy beaches, off which one may prefer to anchor in pleasant surroundings, but the holding here is not reliable.

Sta. Manza has recently become a popular bathing place with a small hotel in the S.E. corner. The shores of the gulf are covered with *maquis*; the N.W. side with its steep cliffs and sandy bays is in contrast to the more gentle slopes rising from the S.E. shore where French campers may now be seen.

Porto Rondinaro is a delightful sandy bay with only one summer villa (1967). A yacht may anchor in 2 to 3 fathom depths on firm sand. The small shallow cove in the northern corner of the bay beyond a rocky spur has 2-fathom depths and shelter all round with a sandy beach close by.

Porto Nuovo, a deserted bay with steep, green, sides and a sandy beach at its head. A creek lies to the southward immediately after the hook of land forming the entrance. Within the creek is good anchorage in 3 fathoms on a sandy bottom; the creek is open only through a narrow sector to N.E.

Porto Sta. Giuglia is a wide inlet with a broad sandy beach, rather too open as a yacht anchorage. The place is now occupied by a Youth Club, sailing schools and campers.

Portovecchio. A large sheltered bay in a magnificent mountainous setting close under an old Corsican town.

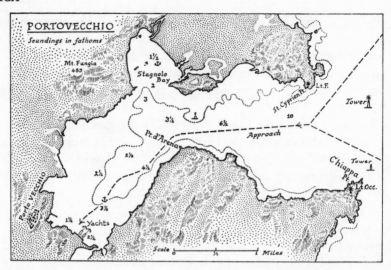

Approach. Chart 1126 and description in Sailing Directions. It can be seen from the plan that the approach either from north or south is straightforward. By night the lights should enable one to reach as far as the inner harbour and then anchor in 2½ fathoms close off the S.E. shore.

Berth. Berth at the head of the harbour, either anchoring where indicated in the plan or secure at the commercial quay (50 yards long); this is often occupied by small coasters; it affords depths of 2½ to 3 fathoms at its extremity, and a yacht can sometimes find room here. The small and rocky inner basin with only 4 to 5 feet depths is not recommended.

Facilities. Unfortunately the port is rather far from the shops which are up the hill inside the old town. If no taxi can be found it will mean a 15-minute walk, but the expedition is worth while for the shops are unusually good. A number of restaurants and some hotels are also in the town. A ship chandler has a shop near the quay. Water is sometimes laid on at the S.E. corner of the quay and there is also a small bar.

The whole setting, together with the old walled town on the hillside (population 3,500), is well worth a visit. It has been praised since earliest times: Diodorus Siculus calls it 'a most beautiful port', Boswell wrote that 'Porto Vecchio may vie with the most distinguished harbour in Europe', and the Sailing Directions of Nelson's day described the harbour as being 'the best in the island, also one of the finest in the Mediterranean; but the badness of the air and the noxious quality of the waters are such that Portovecchio is abandoned and almost useless'. Fortunately this ill has now been remedied by modern methods, and in the town decaying houses have been taken in hand for repairs, and modern shops and restaurants have given the place a new look.

The berthing facilities for a yacht at the port, being so poor, it is recommended that having visited the town a yacht should then go outside to a nearby anchorage. Here, in cool and sheltered conditions, one can better enjoy the fine views of the tall mountain ranges. The following anchorages are suitable:

Stagnolo Bay. One should study the chart to avoid grounding on the extensive banks when approaching. There is good anchorage on a mud bottom N.E. of the above-water rocks in 2½ fathoms. A sailing school and organized camping line the shores. Complete shelter.

St. Cyprien. The next bay northwards is similar though it lacks complete shelter. Anchor west of the island on a sandy bottom.

Pinarello Bay—see Chart 1126—is rather exposed and seems to offer no advantages.

From Portovecchio northwards the coast is almost without shelter until reaching Bastia, 70 miles distant. The first part of the coast being mountainous, a yacht is warned against the strong squalls that sweep down especially during fresh W. to N.W. winds when it is advisable to stand 4 or 5 miles off the coast.

In Roman days there was a river port at Aleria 30 miles northward, with a colony founded by Sulla. Here the Tavignano river has silted and extended its delta; the remains of the Roman settlement have gone, and now there is a small hamlet where a few shallow draught boats are based which enter and leave the present insignificant stream.

Another 25 miles further north, and only 10 miles from Bastia, is the mouth of the Golo River, which has gradually built up an agricultural plain. But today there is no river entrance and there are only a few unimportant ruins at the Roman site of Mariana. Nearby is a 12th-century church which can be visited by road from Bastia.

Bastia. A large and unattractive town standing above a commercial port; hardly interesting enough to merit a special visit.

Approach. Chart 1126, plan. Large yachts make for the commercial port of St. Nicholas; small yachts for the Vieux Port.

Berth. As in sketch-plan with the yacht's stern to the quay. The Vieux Port may be full of fishing craft—shelter good.

Officials. Both Harbour Master and Customs are at the main building of the commercial port.

Facilities. Water at the quays of both the Vieux Port and Commercial Port. A good market takes place daily by the town hall near Place St. Nicholas. There are hotels and several restaurants, some noted for serving good fish dishes. Fuel by tanker—Chantiers Navals for repair work; a mechanical workshop is close at hand. At the small yacht club at the root of the mole showers are obtainable.

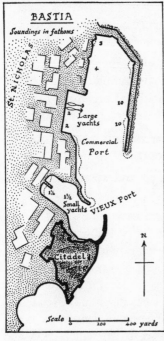

BASTIA

Soundings in fathoms

St. Nicholas

3

4

10

½ Large
¼ yachts 10

Commercial
Port

1¼ 1½
Small
yachts VIEUX Port

N

Citadel

Scale |___|___|___| 400 yards
0   200

Air connections with France and London. Coach tours to the spectacular Corse Peninsula: ferry steamer to Nice three nights a week.

Although no longer the capital of Corsica, Bastia—a town of nearly 55,000 people—still operates the largest port which in summer handles great numbers of French tourists.

When one looks from seaward at the town today it is not easy to imagine the defended walled city that confronted Nelson's ships in 1794. The Vieux Port was the Port of Bastia at that time, and was then referred to in Sailing Directions as 'fit only for galleys and tartans; dangerous puffs of land winds from N.W. Only practical for one ship at once.'

In the massive fortress overlooking the port are relics of Genoese days as well as those of Corsican Patriots. One of the exhibits is a pair of pistols which were always carried by General Paoli.

When Britain was driving out the French from Corsica in 1794 an unsuccessful attempt was made in February to capture Bastia with military support from the British garrison then in San Fiorenzo; a final attempt, mainly by naval assault from seaward, brought about the French surrender on 19th May. After the fall of other ports, Corsica surrendered and the island was administered by Britain for nearly two years. Success in the Mediterranean, however, was followed by British reverses elsewhere and a shattering decision was reached in London that Corsica must be abandoned. When evacuation had been nearly completed, the Viceroy received a despatch telling him of Pitt's decision to rescind this order, but if it was now too late to countermand it on the spot, Elba must be retained instead. 'Do His Majesty's ministers know their own minds?' wrote an exasperated Nelson. On a stormy October night in 1796, the last of the British garrison marched out and with difficulty embarked in ships' boats; nearly a quarter of a million pounds worth of stores were already evacuated and stowed on board the waiting ships. It was blowing a gale at the time and the consequent big swell made boatwork very difficult, for the only shelter was the Vieux Port, and instead of a lighthouse, a watch-tower had been built on its extremity where, according to Sailing Directions, 'a fire could be lit during darkness and bad weather to direct ships into port'. Anchored off

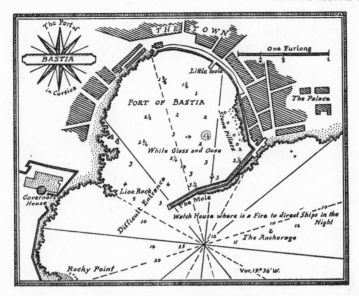

The above plan of the original small port is from a survey made for Nelson's ships.

were H.M.S. *Southampton* and the transports which had already dragged their anchors, while the 'ships boats had never ceased working night or day'. In conclusion Nelson wrote, 'it was dawn of day before the general and myself went into the barge, not one man being left ashore'. Finally the ships weighed and in the strong N. wind soon reached Elba, where they were later joined by the evacuated garrisons of Calvi and Ajaccio. Although it was not anticipated at the time, Elba, too, was shortly to be abandoned, for military commitments in so many parts of the world had placed such a burden on British resources, that it was no longer possible for Britain to maintain herself in the Mediterranean.

Port Macinaggio. A very small and shallow port, attractive and suitable for a small yacht in settled weather.

The following information has been provided by small yachts which have used the harbour:

Approach. Chart 1126, plan. By steering for the breakwater lighthouse on a course W.S.W. one should not encounter depths of less than 8 to 9 feet. (The shoal N.E. of the entrance is shown on plan.) After passing the lighthouse turn southwards, keeping away from the N.W. side of the harbour. In 1969 it was reported that the harbour had been deepened by dredging.

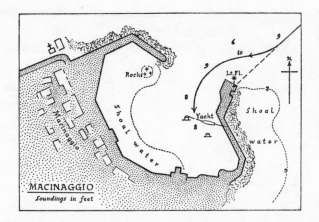

Berth. Secure bows to a buoy and take a warp to the breakwater. Harbour is exposed to winds between N. and E. and can only be recommended in settled weather.

Facilities. Water-tap on the quay. Fresh provisions at a shop in the port. Bus communication with Bastia.

Macinaggio is a pleasant little port used by fishing-craft; the old village of Rogliano with its ruined castle stands on the hill nearby.

Its only record in history was the departure of an expedition of Paoli's to capture Capraia from the Genoese on the 16th February, 1767.

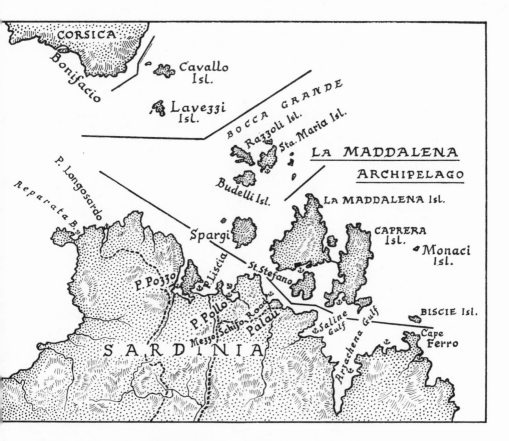

1. PILOTAGE IN THE BONIFACIO STRAIT
Bocca Grande (which divides French territory from Italian)
The Passages between the Islands
South Channel

2. THE ITALIAN ARCHIPELAGO OF LA MADDALENA

Northern Group   Southern Group
  Razzoli Island   La Maddalena Island
  Santa Maria Island   Caprera Island
  Budelli Island   Santo Stefano Island
                   Spargi Island

NOTE. *The French Islands, Cavallo and Lavezzi, with the Piantarella Channel are described in Chapter 2, and the Northern Sardinia ports and anchorages are described in Chapter 4.*

3

The Bonifacio Strait

THE BONIFACIO STRAIT

See Mediterranean Pilot, Vol. I.

Pilotage—This chapter describes the channels through the Bonifacio Strait (which separates Corsica from Sardinia) and also the La Maddalena Archipelago, and refers to the Sardinian anchorages bordering the Strait.

This rocky area of islands and inlets, with its frequent fresh winds, provides a delightful cruising ground for a yacht. Until a very few years ago the southern shores of this fascinating strait were untouched by the spread of modern development and tourism, but even now, thanks to sensible planning, the coast may yet continue to remain largely unspoilt for a few years. About twenty anchorages are described, entirely suitable for the small to medium-sized yacht where there is often good shelter in unspoilt surroundings.

Winds and Current. During summer, winds between S.W. and N.W. have a preponderance, and sometimes blow with strength through the channels. E. winds come second in importance. The current flows in the same direction as the wind, but when the wind changes and starts to blow in the opposite direction, the new current does not always set in at once, and owing to this lag may occasionally be observed flowing in a direction contrary to that of the wind. It is to be felt most strongly in the centre of the Strait and near the shores of Sardinia—off Longosardo—when it sometimes attains a rate of 2–3 knots. Winds from N. and S. also occur, but not nearly so frequently as the N.W. and E. winds. Although the wind strength in the summer months does not normally exceed that of fresh or occasionally strong, a single gale has been known to occur in recent years during the month of July. Strong winds from the N.W. set up a long sea; those from N.E. and E. a much shorter one.

Details of the Piantarella Channel have already been given on page 46. Now comes the broad, main steamer channel which is also the Franco-Italian frontier:

Bocca Grande, of 3 miles navigable width (described in Vol. I of Sailing Directions) presents no difficulties. Referring to sailing yachts, an earlier edition states 'all sorts of vessels can go through without fear, although the sea is sometimes very high there with a prodigious roaring'.

The Southern Channel is 3 cables wide and is easy to negotiate. It is often used by yachts and small vessels on passage between the Maddalena Islands and the east coast of Sardinia. Cape Ferro is high, steep-to and well lit; by night, especially if beating to windward through this channel, one must beware of the underwater rocks on the S.E. of Biscie Island.

A notable record of this passage being used by large sailing vessels occurred on 20th January, 1805, when Nelson, during darkness, led his eleven ships from the Agincourt anchorage to sea. See page 66.

The other channels giving access between the E. and W. sides of the strait are seldom used and do not merit a description.

LA MADDALENA ARCHIPELAGO

The seven principal islands are:

Razzoli, Santa Maria and Budelli in the Northern Group.
La Maddalena, Caprera, Santo Stefano and Spargi in the Southern Group.

The three Northern Islands—once called the Barelino Islands—have some useful anchorages for yachts, especially with N.E. winds. With the exception of Budelli the islands are barren.

Island of Razzoli

(a) **Cala Lunga.** During the approach one must be careful to avoid off-lying rocks, both above and below water. Beyond a hook of land on the N. side is a mooring buoy and just beyond this a small yacht may anchor on a bottom of sand and boulders in depths of 2 fathoms. The shelter is all-round, but the holding uncertain.

(b) **Cala Giorgio Marina** provides good shelter and plenty of space to manœuvre. Anchor close under the N. shore one mile from the outcrops of rocks on the N. side of the entrance. Near the anchorage is an underwater rock, but this is normally visible through the clear water.

Island of Santa Maria. The shallow bay on the S. side affords excellent anchorage in 2 fathoms off a long sandy beach. A few summer villas have grown up above the beach overlooking the turquoise blue water in the bay.

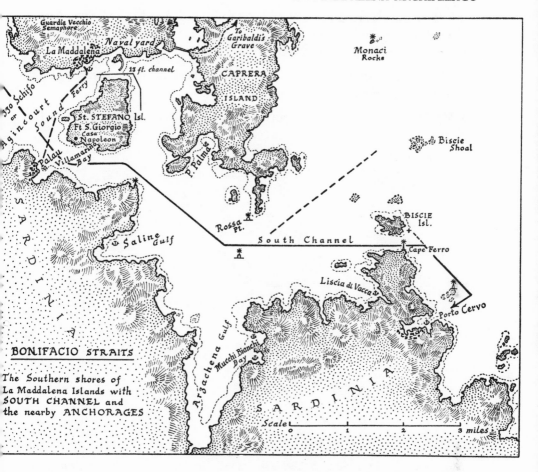

The mooring buoy placed in the middle of the bay belongs to the Italian Navy. There are no facilities and even water must be ferried across from Sardinia.

Island of Budelli has a cove with a sandy bottom on the S. side by a spur where small yachts sometimes anchor, and another little cove on the S.E.

These islands consist of granite rock, and are without water or vegetation. The few summer visitors get their water and supplies in small freighters from Sardinia.

The four Southern Islands, with the capital and port of La Maddalena, lie close off the indented Sardinian coast which benefits from the shelter they help to provide.

All these islands are composed of red granite and largely covered in scrub, and in the clear blue waters of the Tyrrhenian Sea this archipelago forms a delightful cruising-ground for yachts.

Island of La Maddalena. On the south side of the island is the attractive little sea-port of the same name.

La Maddalena is the most important place in the Bonifacio Straits, with reasonable shelter and facilities for yachts.

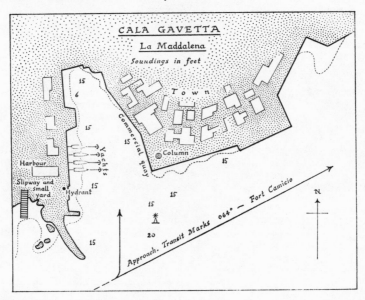

The Port

Approach. Charts 564 and 2157. Yachts should make for Cala Gavetta. Approaching along Radi de Maddalena one follows the leading marks below Fort Camicio (in transit 064°). Conspicuous stone obelisks and buoys mark all obstructions on the north side of the channel. The naval school stands out well on the rising ground behind the port, and by night there are leading lights, all fully described in Sailing Directions.

Berth. There are depths of 3½ fathoms towards the middle of Cala Gavetta and by the quays 2 fathoms except in the N.W. corner where the water shoals. The most convenient place to berth is off the first or second stone bollard. (A shallow rock marked by a small white buoy may be passed close either side.) Shelter has been much improved by the recent extension of the mole from the S.W. corner of the basin. The commercial quay, too, has been extended southwards.

Officials. Harbour Master and Customs. Naval and military commandants.

Facilities. The town is close to the quay, and has an excellent market, and good shops, all supplies coming from Sardinia. A new Telegraph Office and Post Office near the main square. A number of restaurants and three hotels. Water, brought from Sardinia, is laid on by hydrants at the quay. There are half a dozen ship chandlers and a small boatyard which can be of service to a yacht.

La Maddalena, a busy and attractive little town of about 10,000 people, maintains a relatively high standard largely due to the naval base. The countryside, mostly of granite rock, has cultivated valleys of vines and corn. A causeway joins La Maddalena to the adjacent island, Caprera. At the church, the memory of Nelson is still preserved: in recognition of the kindness shown by the people of the town to the sailors of the British Fleet when based here in 1804, Nelson presented to the church a pair of silver candlesticks and a cross. They may still be seen today. At this time La Maddalena was not the healthy place it is now, for we read of Nelson directing his captains' attention to the 'very great danger attending the health of seamen sent in "wooding and watering" parties, either to the island of Sardinia or the Maddalena Islands, which abound with marshes'; the purser was to supply the surgeon 'with two gills of wine or one gill of spirits per day for each of the men sent on shore—to be mixed with Peruvian-bark'.

Island of Caprera, joined to La Maddalena, is about the same size and although partially fertile is little inhabited; the only interest is the house and tomb of Garibaldi. After his historic transformation of Italy and his adventures in South America, Garibaldi came to Caprera to spend the remainder of his life in exile. He died here in 1882, twenty years later, and was buried in the garden close beside his flat-roofed bungalow, Casa Bianca. His daughter, Donna Clelia, lived on there, and until 1958 would welcome visitors, replying in excellent French to any questions they might have to ask about her father's life. She had preserved his room as he had left it on his death, decorated with vivid reminders of a patriotic and adventurous life; the red shirt worn in the assault on Sicily, the saddle of his old horse, Marsala, and many old and faded photographs. Now Donna Clelia is dead, buried beside the graves of her parents and her two sisters, and the house is preserved as a memorial by the Italian government. A taxi can reach the house by the island's only road in about twenty minutes.

Close northward of Casa Bianca is **Port Garibaldi,** with a shallow anchorage open to the north. Club Mediterranée has a sailing school here. On Caprera's south coast is **Porto Palma**, a military area and in any case unsuitable for a yacht. But west of Isolotto Porco is an anchorage shown on the Admiralty Chart. Here one can shelter from most winds close under a short pier. (Its extremity is lit at night.) The depths are convenient and the bottom is sand.

61

Island of Santo Stefano, separated from La Maddalena by a 13-foot channel, is barren and is used only for oil storage and for quarrying stone. On the south side a distinctive fort, S. Giorgio, stands close above the narrow inlet of Cala di Villamarina. This inlet is no longer of interest to a yacht because the northern end has been blocked by a causeway used in connection with the quarry workings.

Island of Spargi, the fourth of the group, is rugged and fringed with rocks. On either side of the southern tip of the island is a cove:

(a) **Arga Bay** (on the W. side), a mediocre small yacht anchorage; but dangerous with underwater rocks, and inconvenient because of a valley through which the N. wind is apt to rush upon yachts at anchor.

(b) **Corsara Bay** (on the E. side), is both suitable and attractive, having convenient depths for anchoring on a sandy bottom. Many yachts find it a pleasant day anchorage.

Lying 500 yards S.W. are the Corsara Rocks with 10-foot depths and marked by a lighted buoy. Great interest was aroused in 1958 when among these rocks was discovered the wreck of a laden 150-ton Roman freighter. This was carefully surveyed by Italian archaeologists and divers; during two seasons of salvage operations in this clear water altogether about three hundred amphorae and other objects were recovered, many being identified by the stamps with their Greek characters. The wreck, buried in sand, was gradually uncovered and carefully photographed so that the keel, stern and frames could be accurately measured for laying off on the drawing board. One interesting fact was that the copper nails which secured the lead sheathing to the hull were themselves coated with lead to preserve them from electrolysis. To sum up, this remarkable discovery revealed the first constructional details of a 100-foot 1st-century B.C. Roman freighter.

Immediately across the narrow strait and lying on the Sardinian shores are the following ports:

Mezzo Schifo Road or Agincourt Sound
Palau
Saline Gulf
Arzachena Gulf
Liscia di Vacca

All are described in the chapter on Sardinia—pages 77–78.

THE BONIFACIO STRAIT IN NELSON'S DAY

It must be of interest to the modern yacht exploring Bonifacio Strait with the detailed charts of today to know something of how the old sailing ships got on when pilotage information was greatly lacking.

The Master's log of H.M.S. *Victory* can be examined among the Public Records, but nothing can be learnt of the sources of his information of local pilotage. There were no lights exhibited in these waters at that time; they were set up half a century later, and the best information available for H.M. ships were the charts supplied officially by one of the London chandlery firms. They had sometimes been corrected, but only partially, from hydrographical information by French and Italian surveyors. This had been augmented by occasional drafts such as that on page 53 and from knowledge imparted by local pilots. Thus in the Corsica–Sardinia area British charts were later described as 'miserable things', and even with information derived from local sources pilotage information was far from accurate. Nelson's ships were frequently putting to sea during this period and returning to one of the Bonifacio anchorages, but apart from one mishap—see page 65—all hazards were missed. Admiral Keats on meeting Nelson later was heard to say; 'It is evident, my Lord, that Providence protects you.'

Seamen of this period evidently learnt to accept great losses of ships through hazards at sea. One may read that more than 500 ships under the English flag were lost every year, largely due to inaccurate surveys and lack of pilotage information. These losses by shipwreck were eight times those of vessels captured or sunk by the enemy or lost by fire. In the year 1820, a bad year for shipwreck, Lloyds estimated that the country lost 677 ships; but by this time a start had been made on naval surveys, for the waters of the United Kingdom, the Mediterranean and North America were now being properly charted.

The discovery of Mezzo Schifo or Agincourt Sound, which serves little purpose for the ordinary yacht today, proved to be a most useful anchorage for Nelson's squadron during the Napoleonic wars when a large French fleet lay at Toulon closely watched by a screen of British frigates.

Still called Agincourt Sound on French charts and on some of the English ones, it was first surveyed by the captain of H.M.S. *Agincourt* shortly before the arrival of the fleet—'One of the best harbours I have ever seen' was the Admiral's opinion at that time. When Nelson brought the fleet here from the offing of Toulon on 31st October, 1803, it was during foul weather—'We worked *Victory* every inch of the way', he wrote, 'from Asinara to this anchorage, the wind blowing from Longosardo, under double-reefed topsails.'

Although Minorca would probably have been a better base for the British ships-of-the-line, this island had only recently been handed over to Spain at the Treaty of Amiens. The newly-found anchorage in the Bonifacio Strait, 200 miles from the enemy, was therefore the nearest and best base for Nelson's ships when in need of supplies. Here they could be quickly alerted by the frigates if the French were to put to sea from Toulon.

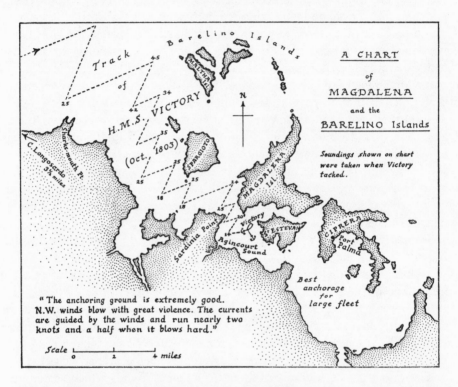

A CHART
of
MAGDALENA
and the
BARELINO Islands

Soundings shown on chart were taken when Victory tacked.

"The anchoring ground is extremely good. N.W. winds blow with great violence. The currents are guided by the winds and run nearly two knots and a half when it blows hard."

Best anchorage for large fleet

Scale

0   2   4 miles

This tracing from the original track made by the Master of H.M.S. *Pearl*, was kindly made available by the Hydrographer of the Navy. It shows *Victory*'s track and the soundings taken whilst tacking during her hard beat against strong south-easterly winds towards the anchorage in Agincourt Sound. Here she can be seen moored 'with best bower to S.E.'.

The names of the islands and places are shown as they were in Nelson's day and it can be seen that, although the coastline is drawn inaccurately, *Victory*'s soundings are mostly correct by today's chart. Other soundings, which were shown on the survey, have not been copied on the above tracing as it would have presented a confusing impression. This chart should be compared with the modern Chart 2157 [see page 59] when it may be seen that the shoals of Biscie (Biche) and Pecora, all with depths of 15 or 16 feet, and Monaci, 9 feet, are not shown, nor yet the Tre Monti shoal in Arzachena Sound which was then recommended as a fleet anchorage.

After the fleet had watered and provisioned in October 1803, it subsequently put to sea, beating out of the Channel north of Biscie Island without mishap, no doubt deriving comfort from the captain of *Agincourt*'s assuring notation on the chart: 'Having been through the passages in a boat after a very heavy gale of wind from S.E. with an extremely high sea, I am convinced that all danger shows itself.' When the fleet returned, however, by the same passage out of which they had beaten, they learnt of the existence of the Monaci shoal when, at 8.15 a.m. on 20th May, H.M.S. *Excellent*, drawing 23 feet 3 inches, 'struck the ground and stuck fast'. She was fortunate in being able to summon all the boats of the squadron to lighten her and to lay out anchors. After 'firing several guns' she got off, and before dusk was leading the squadron through the Barellino Passage into Agincourt Sound.

Although British charts did not show these hazards, the Maltese pilots apparently knew of their existence and, apart from *Excellent*'s mishap, the British fleet during these fifteen months when working from this base must have had remarkable escapes from disaster.

On 20th January, 1805 a dramatic event occurred when, on a wintry afternoon, with gales from the N.W., as Nelson's fleet lay at anchor at Agincourt

Copy of the portion of a chart by Captain Ryves, H.M.S. Agincourt, with estimated track of H.M.S. Victory leading the squadron to sea in January 1805
(*Owing to the small scale reproduction, only soundings near Victory's track have been inserted.*)

Sound the frigates *Active* and *Seahorse* were sighted coming from the west-ward, evidently as look-outs from Toulon. They were flying the long-expected signal 'Enemy at sea'. Within one and a half hours Nelson's ships had unmoored and were putting to sea, but with the strong W.N.W. wind blowing they could only sail eastwards out of the Strait, having to pass during darkness through the narrow Biscie* Passage scarcely 600 yards wide. With *Victory* leading, they entered this channel at 6 p.m., each ship burning a stern-light and following the next ahead. At 6.34 *Victory* burnt a blue light followed by another ten minutes later. Soon all eleven ships and two frigates had safely passed through and entered the Tyrrhenian Sea, and at 7.15 they hove-to on the star-board tack to enable *Seahorse* to close *Victory* for the captain to come on board. He was directed by Nelson to proceed ahead of the fleet towards the islet of Toro and there seek intelligence of the French fleet. Nelson's ships had left Agincourt Sound for the last time: they had started on the 'long chase' which culminated in the Battle of Trafalgar.

* Now called South Channel.

SARDINIA

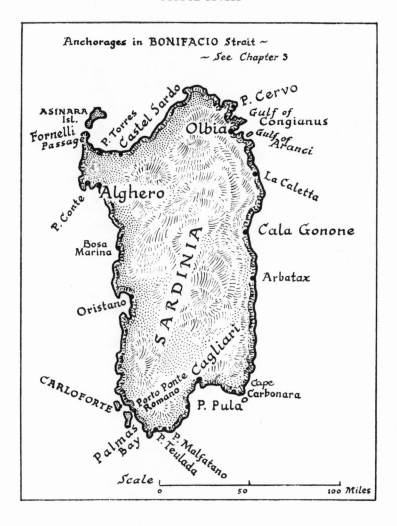

Anchorages in BONIFACIO Strait ~
~ See Chapter 3

ASINARA Isl.
P. Cervo
Gulf of Congianus
Castel Sardo
P. Torres
Olbia
Fornelli Passage
Gulf of Aranci
La Caletta
Alghero
P. Conte
Cala Gonone
Bosa Marina
SARDINIA
Arbatax
Oristano
Cagliari
CARLOFORTE
Porto Ponte Romano
Cape Carbonara
P. Pula
Palmas Bay
P. Malfatano
P. Teulada

Scale
0   50   100 Miles

Bonifacio Strait
(Northern Ports opposite La Maddalena)
Santa Reparata
Longosardo or Santa Teresa
Porto Pozzo
Marmorata Bay
Porto Liscia
Porto Pollo
Mezzo Schifo Sound
Palau
Saline Gulf
Cala Mucchi Bianchi
Arzachena Gulf
Liscia di Vacca

East Coast
Porto Cervo
Gulf of Congianus
Cala di Volpe
Golfo di Cognena
Porto Rotondo
Golfo di Marinella
Golfo Aranci
Olbia
Island of Tavolara
Porto San Paolo
Porto Taverna
Cala Coda Cavallo
Porto Brandinghi
La Caletta
Cala Gonone
Arbatax
Port Giunco

South Coast
Carbonara Bay Anchorages
Pinocchio Tower Anchorage
Cagliari
Capo Pula Anchorage
Torre Chia Anchorage
Port Malfatano
Port Teulada
Port Scudo
Cala Brigantina

South-west Coast
Gulf of Palmas
Piombo Bay
Porto Pino
Porto Botte
Porto Ponte Romano
Island of Sant'Antioco
Calasetta
Island of San Pietro
Carloforte

West Coast
Oristano
Bosa Marina
Alghero
Porto Conte
Fornelli Passage and Island of Asinara
Port Torres
Castel Sardo

4

Sardinia

INTRODUCTION

'A rugged wild country, but in large part contains much fertile land, rich in all kinds of produce and most especially corn.'   STRABO

Sardinia, three times the size of Corsica, also has high mountains, rising abruptly on the east coast and sloping away to the west, with a covering of maquis and a considerable woodland of scrub-oak and pine. The population is now more than one and a half million, some being of Genoese extraction speaking a form of Italian, others, especially in the interior, are of Sardinian origin. The west side of the island is the most populated, many being employed in agriculture, some in the mines, others in growing cotton, fruit and wine, and in fishery. The standard of living generally is lower than on the Italian mainland.

The early Sards who lived here during the Bronze Age period built a large number of *nuraghi* (fortified dwellings constructed between 1500 and 500 B.C.): bronze figures, and tools, reveal how these people lived. Later Phoenician settlements were established in the S.W. to work the mines. When the Romans came they made the island productive: corn was grown and exported to Italy; lead, antimony, iron, copper and silver were mined. Nothing material is left to remind one of the Romans; they hated the Sards and although Roman troops were sent to preserve order and suppress banditary, they were unable to civilize the people. Centuries later, after periodical raids by Vandals and others, came the Pisans, followed by the Aragonese; they both built churches, some of which still survive.

In the interior, the people of today are the descendants of the original Sards, and they behave not unlike the Sicilians in continuing family feuds and stealing. Lately the conduct of the mountain inhabitants has deteriorated and in recent years there were fifty to a hundred unsolved murders annually and many kidnappings. Police action has been ineffective in stamping out crime, and meanwhile banditry has become so active that hostages have been taken even from coastal villages. On the plains much has been achieved by improving agriculture, and the establishment of a co-operative movement has met with success.

The potentialities of tourism have been realized, and a few years ago a blaze of publicity ushered in the Costa Smeralda and made it one of the most fashionable yachting resorts of the Mediterranean. At one or two places on the coast some modern hotels have been built—perhaps the best known being Alghero, a Catalan town where the old blends quite happily with the new. This development of the coastal fringe is in striking contrast to the interior where life continues in the ways which have prevailed for centuries.

Regarding the fauna in Sardinia, one hears of the wild horses of the Giari di Gusturi and the white donkeys of Asinara; but of wild life today, the stag and mouflon, described by Pliny and Strabo, are now protected, and there are boar, hare, rabbits and partridges, but very few birds; eagles are indigenous, and flamingoes and pelicans, sometimes seen on the lagoons, are migratory.

Communications

Passenger Ferries:
Civitavecchia–Olbia (every night)
Civitavecchia–Cagliari (every night)
Naples–Cagliari (twice a week)
Palermo–Cagliari (weekly)
Genoa–Porto Torres (every night)
Bonifacio–S. Teresa di Gallura (daily, Sundays excepted—twice a day in summer)
Cagliari–Tunis (fortnightly)

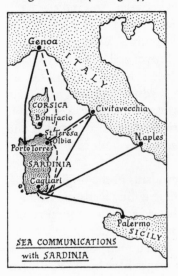

SEA COMMUNICATIONS with SARDINIA

Car Ferries run from:
Civitavecchia to Golfo Aranci (twice daily)
Also another service from Genoa to Olbia and Cagliari
There is also a daily ferry service between Sardinia and Corsica:
Port Torres, Palau, La Maddalena and Bonifacio

Air Connections:
From Alghero and Cagliari to Rome several times daily.
Internally there is frequent air connection between Cagliari and Alghero.

Internal Rail Services:
The railway network covers much of the island and bus services connect the coastal towns and villages.

The Coast. Sardinia has more than a thousand miles of coastline. The number of both safe and agreeable ports suitable for a yacht are few, but during settled weather there are some delightful places with sufficient shelter for a short stay. The most attractive areas for the cruising yacht are the Bonifacio Strait and the N.E. Coast (Costa Smeralda); but there are also a number of anchorages, especially on the S.W. and some distantly separated ports, which are safe and agreeable, such as Cagliari, Carloforte and Alghero.

Weather. The tall mountains influence the strength and direction of the wind in different localities. On the west coast during the summer months its direction is mainly from the N.W., and it is also N.W. in the Gulf of Cagliari. On the east coast it is variable according to the configuration of the coast. There are frequent calms, and occasional E. or S.E. winds, humid and oppressive, when a depression passes.

Weather forecasts may be obtained on 1,578–1,331 metres—6,060 kc/s at 5.35 and 13.55 (G.M.T.).

The coast is often obscured by haze and a yacht may find it difficult to identify her landfall. The air and sea beacons shown on page 21 can be most helpful.

Food and Wine. At most of the tourist restaurants one can get the normal Italian cooking. The following seafish dishes are often served: *orata* (gilthead), *dentice* (sea-bream), *spigola* (bass), *cefalo* (grey mullet), *sogliolo* (sole), *triglia* (red mullet), *merluzzo* (hake), occasionally *trotta* (trout), also *gamberoni* (prawns), *aragosta* (crawfish) and *frutta di mare* (sea food). Fish is often to be recommended rather than the somewhat tough meat. In the country villages, even among the poorer ones, there are a number of local dishes much praised by Italians from the mainland.

The Sardinian wines are strong, dark in colour, and sometimes too sweet. White wine appears like a rosé and red is almost black. The situation however is likely to improve in the course of years, for the new co-operative movement has already begun to replant some of the older vineyards with better vines more likely to please discerning customers.

At Cagliari a palatable red wine comes from the Campirodano Plain, N.W. of the town. At Oristano a popular Vernaccia wine is sold, the years '57 to '60 being particularly good. This wine, produced in a large quantity, has now become a brand under the co-operative, and is sold everywhere as 'Sardinian Gold'. A reasonably good aperitif is also called Vernaccia; it is unfortified, rather dry and something like sherry.

Tunny nets are often a serious obstruction to the sailing yacht and under certain conditions it is difficult to judge how far to seaward one must go to

71

clear the end of the nets. Both Sailing Directions and charts refer to the laying of these nets which, being a seasonal operation, deserves further description.

Tunny fishing was a Phoenician industry, and was continued in the Mediterranean by the Romans, especially in Sardinia, where *Saltamentum Sardicum* was the much appreciated 'salted tunny' at the fish markets in Rome. At this time the fish was merely packed in salt, obtained locally, before shipment to the mainland; but today the process is more elaborate. On being landed, the fish are cut up and cleaned in salt water, then soaked in olive oil before being transferred to barrels for sterilizing and eventual shipment. In Europe nowadays tunny are caught on lines in the Bay of Biscay, in circular nets in the North Adriatic, but off Sardinia and Sicily in long lines of net extending at right angles from certain points on the coast.

Every year in mid-March preparations for the tunny season are begun. Genoese fishermen arrive and start preparing the *mattanza*—the long widemesh net barrier, laid vertically, more than a mile in length, very deep at its outer end and secured by many anchors to the sea-bed; this is prepared during the course of the next few weeks. Its purpose, when laid, is to deflect the fish from their normal easterly course (migrating towards the Black Sea) towards the T of the net, where their doom is eventually sealed.

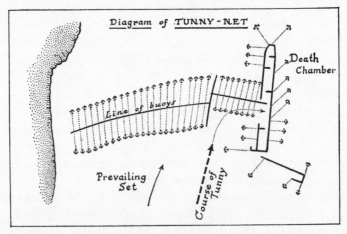

At the cross of the T is another arrangement of nets in the form of 'rooms' leading into the final 'room' with a rising 'floor'—the *camera de la morte*—alongside which are moored open lighters.

The laying of this arrangement of nets (the *incrocciatura*) with its many anchors takes about six weeks, and is supervised by the headman. By the beginning of May all is ready and priests are brought in to bless the nets. Any time in the first week of May the first shoals of tunny are sighted and the fishermen are alerted to row off and man their lighters at the death chamber. When the headman considers sufficient fish have entered the death chamber, the 'door' is closed and the bottom drawn up. As the surface is reached, these gigantic fish rush madly around snorting and jostling one another in their frenzy to escape. The men plunge long spikes into the bodies and the sea becomes a blood-bath. With large gaffs and knives they drag these struggling monsters into the lighters which, together with the men, are soon covered in an ever-increasing flow of blood. To quieten the struggling fish during this operation, one of the men sometimes presses his hand over the eye; this apparently has the immediate effect of eliminating their exertions. The occasional swordfish sometimes enters the net with the tunny and has to be tackled separately by securing its tail.

The British Interest. Sardinia was not generally regarded as being of strategic importance to the great powers until Nelson brought it into the limelight.

When the British fleet, based in the Bonifacio Strait, was blockading the French at Toulon in 1804, Nelson made repeated attempts to persuade the British government to seize the island. Writing to Lord Hobart from *Victory* at Agincourt Sound on 22nd December, 1804, Nelson continued: 'if we could possess one island, Sardinia, we should want neither Malta nor any other; this which is the finest island in the Mediterranean possesses harbours fit for arsenals and of a capacity to hold our Navy within 24 hours sail of Toulon'. In a letter to Lord Hawkesbury, he claimed that Sardinia was 'worth fifty Maltas'. Other letters in a similar strain had also been written to influential members of the government; but very little heed was paid to Nelson's persuasions. Apart from the main anchorage near La Maddalena, where the fleet was maintained, Nelson's ships had at various times anchored at Aranci Bay, Pula, Palmas Bay, Carloforte and Oristano where sometimes food and water had been obtained and live sheep, bullocks, and wine had been purchased. The fleet had also been well replenished from storeships which had made a rendezvous at these places after being convoyed from Gibraltar and Malta. Although conversant with the nature of the ports, Nelson knew nothing of the island, for during this long period he never stepped ashore.

Half a century later the British were to see more of the Sardinians: fighting beside them at the Crimea were two brigades commanded by General della Marmora. The *Armata Sarda* was well thought of, being described by the army's special correspondent as 'excellent and soldier-like troops. . . . The officers were well mounted, and everyone admired the air and carriage of the troops, more especially of the *Bersaglieri*, and the eye was attracted by their melodramatic head-dress—a bandit-looking hat with a large plume of black cock's feathers in the side.'

Ancient Remains. There are dolmen (similar to those found in Malta) mega-lithic tombs, and standing stones; but the most interesting and characteristic of Sardinia are the Bronze Age examples of fortified dwellings and defences called *nuraghe* (about 1500 B.C. to 500 B.C.).

'Nuraghi ~ St. Sabina

More than six thousand of these conical towers have been found in various states of preservation. Built throughout a long period of more than a thousand years, their purpose was originally to shelter the inhabitants of the larger farm-steads. Later they developed into complicated fortifications housing perhaps two hundred to three hundred men. *Nuraghe* are almost entirely to be found at inland sites some distance from the sea at altitudes of 500 to 1,000 feet. A number of these, as well as tombs, sacred wells etc. can be visited quite con-veniently by car from the following ports:

Alghero—'Palmavera', a *nuraghi*, off the road to P. Conti.

Arzachena—a *nuraghi* stronghold at Cabu Abbas.

Aranci—a *nuraghi* well.

Cagliari—Caves on Capo Sant'Elia, Barumini and Isili.

Cape Pula—The ancient site of Nora.

Porto Ponte Romano—The site of Sulcis on Sant'Antioco Island.

(*Sardinia* by Margaret Guido (Thames & Hudson) should be studied for detailed information.)

Pilotage Information—See *Mediterranean Pilot*, Vol. I.

NORTH COAST

The Sardinian ports lying on the Bonifacio Strait become more of interest to a yacht when reaching the shelter afforded by La Maddalena Archipelago.

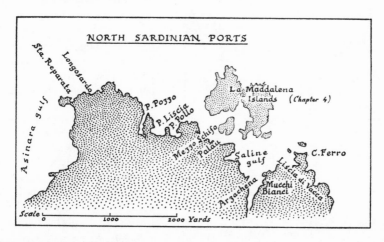

Santa Reparata. A small deserted bay, sometimes of interest as a place of shelter.

> **Approach.** Charts 2157 and 1189. To avoid the shoal patches off the western headland it is advisable to keep near the eastern shore.
>
> **Anchorage.** With the prevailing N.W. wind one should anchor near the weather shore, where the bottom is rather uneven with clusters of heavy weed on patches of clear sand in convenient depths. With the wind in this quarter a swell comes into the bay and the wind blows fairly hard over the low land.
>
> **Facilities.** There is nothing to be obtained close at hand, there being only a couple of farms and some small houses. Sta. Teresa is the nearest village which is connected by a road leading over the hill. On the western side of the bay is a sandy beach steep-to and good for bathing. No doubt it will soon be developed.

The next port, Longosardo, often called after its village Santa Teresa, the main Sardinian terminal in the north, is far better sheltered than Sta. Reparata.

Longosardo or Santa Teresa. A long unspoilt inlet with a ferry-port; also used by coastal craft. There is good shelter inside.

> **Approach.** Chart 1189. The off-lying shoals are marked by buoys and the rock awash is clearly visible. Both the western tower and the white light tower on Pta. Corvo are conspicuous and make the approach easy even if the buoys should not be watching. The new buildings on the western side of the entrance are now more conspicuous than the old tower. Once inside the shoals one may steer for the steamer quay.

SANTA TERESA
(LONGOSARDO)

Soundings in fathoms

Scale 0 100 200 300 yards

Berth off the quay on the west side of the port as far south as draught permits, or one may ride to an anchor. The holding is firm mud and the shelter good, except for winds between N. and N.E., when it is essential to lay out a kedge to hold up the bows.

Facilities. Nothing to be obtained in the port, but 1 mile up the hill is the village of Sta. Teresa, where most things can be bought. There is also a Jolly Hotel and one or two restaurants. From here a motor-road connects with other places on the island. The ferry steamer from here to La Maddalena and Bonifacio calls daily, and also in summer a car ferry, both of which take up space at the same quay. (The boat slip in the S. corner of the quay is suitable only for local boats.) A daily bus runs to Alghero.

Officials. At the new Harbour Office and Customs House, officials are usually interested in Ship's Papers.

The village was named after Queen Maria Teresa when a colony of Piedmontese was established here in the 19th century by the King of Sardinia. The port is often called after the village, although the older generation prefer the original name of Longosardo. (The recent Sailing Directions (Vol. I, 1963) spells the name Longonsardo.)

Marmorata Bay, open to N.E. but well sheltered from other quarters. There is anchorage in 2–3 fathom depths, and a sandy bathing beach close by. N.W. winds sometimes send in a swell.

Porto Pozzo has a straightforward approach down the centre of the channel, leading to the anchorage in about 3 fathoms.

Porto Liscia, a pleasant deserted anchorage with good shelter and holding.

Approach and Anchorage. Charts 2157, 1189. After entering the cove make for the western end of the sandy beach and anchor in 5–6 fathoms, 300 yards from the most southerly rocks. The small bridge may be seen in line with the sand. Except with northerly winds, the shelter is adequate and the holding on blue clay is good. Some yachts prefer the eastern side of the cove which although exposed to the north, has good holding ground and affords more room to swing.

Sailing ships used to call here to fill their casks from a spring in the S.W. corner of the bay.

Porto Pollo, a pleasant, well-sheltered, natural harbour. One may anchor behind a small islet (N.E. of 5 fathom sounding on the chart) near some sandy patches, which are delightful places for bathing.

Continuing eastward it may be seen on the next map that the following anchorages lie close southward of La Maddalena Islands from which they derive much shelter. The coast shown on Chart 2157 should therefore be studied when planning to cruise in the Bonifacio Strait.

Mezzo Schifo Sound. In the S.W. corner of this sound a cluster of villas has grown up, and now motor-yachts sometimes anchor off. A short protecting mole has been built to shelter the smaller power-boats.

Palau is a shallow inlet with sufficient shelter at its entrance for the Maddalena ferry-boat to berth at the quay.

A village is now growing up where formerly only transport, police, customs and railway officials were accommodated for duties concerned with the ferry to and from La Maddalena. Part of the quay is reserved by the naval and military authority, but the shoreward side, which is shallow, provides shelter for local *tartanes* and fishing craft.

Train and bus services in conjunction with La Maddalena ferry connect with Sassari and Alghero.

Saline Gulf is a pleasant place to anchor in all except easterly winds. Off the northern shore one may let go in 3–4 fathoms on a bottom of weed on sand. The place is attractive, with the granite shore mostly covered by bush or scrub, and very few dwellings to be seen.

Cala Mucchi Bianchi (in the Arzachena Gulf) is one of the more attractive anchorages in the Bonifacio Strait.

Approach. Chart 2157. The two rocks awash are clearly shown on the chart and are easily avoided. The northern bay is the more suitable anchorage.

Anchorage. There are 3-fathom depths inside the line of the small stone quay, and shelter is very reasonable.

Facilities. Only a few villas have been set up, but further building is planned; already hotels have been opened in the vicinity, but just out of sight from the anchorage.

Towards the head of the **Arzachena Gulf** there is no shelter suitable for a yacht; Cannigonni, the conspicuous small village, has now become a holiday place with Youth Hostel and small hotel.

Eastward, beyond Cape Tre Monti, villas have grown up, and a substantial pier now extends from the centre of Battistone Bay.

Liscia di Vacca attracts a few motor-yachts to its rather indifferent anchorage because of the recently constructed hotel and a number of modern villas close to the shore. Except in fine weather it is not recommended for smaller yachts; moreover, the sea-bed near the shore has a number of underwater rocks. The most suitable anchorage for a yacht is in the S.E. corner where, in depths of 5 fathoms, the sea-bed is of sand.

EAST COAST

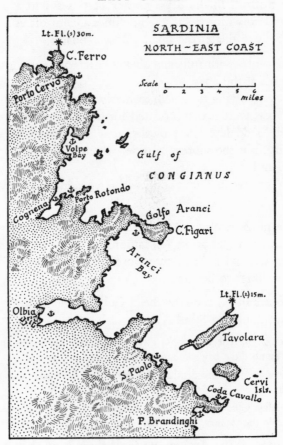

The Costa Smeralda on the N.E. coast is the popular cruising area for every kind of yacht, and until ten years ago this beautiful coast was quite unblemished

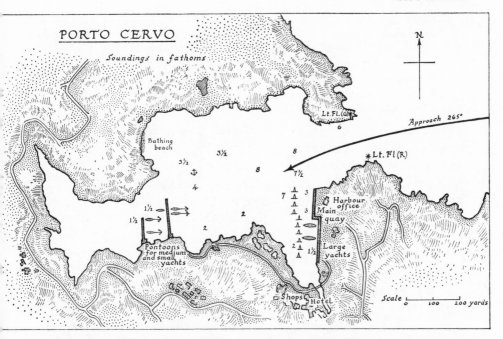

by modern buildings. It has now been 'developed', though not entirely spoilt from the point of view of the visiting yachtsman. One or two of the modern yacht ports are very well set up and pleasant for a short stay among up-to-date surroundings. A few anchorages are still untouched and one can find shelter tucked into the dramatic mountainous coves of Sardinia.

Porto Cervo. A beautiful, well-enclosed bay, now transformed into a select and efficient yacht haven with every facility.

Approach. Charts 1189, 163. Cervo Shoal is now indicated by a large white Landfall buoy. The entrance to Porto Cervo indicated by two leading marks on the hill on a bearing 265°, is less than a cable wide, and is marked by the usual flashing red and green harbour lights set upon small white pedestals.

Berth. (a) A substantial quay for *large yachts*, 250 metres in length, with depths of 10 feet (inner end) and 24 feet (outer end) lies on the port hand; yachts berth stern to the quay, bows being secured by warps to the mooring buoys—a club boat is in attendance. Fresh water, electricity (220–110, 12 and 24 volts), and sometimes telephones are laid on at this quay.

(b) **Medium size and smaller yachts** may berth in a similar manner at long pontoons reaching from the southern shore, where fresh water is also laid on. E.N.E. winds send in a small swell, but on the whole shelter is excellent all round. In the centre of the inlet there is normally space to swing to an anchor in convenient depths over a bottom of mud or sand, and here no one bothers you.

Facilities. As well as fresh water, at the berth there are facilities for fuel (duty free); a yachting outfitter, supermarket, bank, restaurant, hotel and night-club all nearby. Foreign newspapers can be bought. Ice is delivered by van—a laundry collects and delivers twice a day. Refuse must be placed in the waste-bins by the quay, and nothing may be thrown overboard. Taxis are available for Olbia or the airport.

Officials. Harbour Master and Customs, whose office is near the main quay. (Stores in transit may be cleared and collected by the yacht.)

This inlet, without habitation only two or three years ago, has now been transformed into the most up-to-date yacht haven in the Mediterranean. At the same time, these modern developments have advanced in good taste, the buildings and installations blending harmoniously into the landscape. Founded by a consortium headed by the Aga Khan, their land is scattered along 35 miles of this indented coast, hitherto unpopulated, and on these shores they are said to have planned to build over a period of fifteen years, many hotels and a few thousand villas. Five hotels have been built and about two hundred villas sold.

The attractive mountainous **Gulf of Congianus** (see Chart 3914) has a number of agreeable anchorages suitable for yachts:

Cala di Volpe is a shallow inlet with good anchorage at its mouth and sheltered except from S.E. Anchor N.W. of some protruding rocks. Landing may be made by dinghy at an expensive pink-washed summer hotel at the head of the shallow creek. A new road passes by here from Olbia towards Porto Cervo and the place is much frequented by Italian yachts. Good bathing in some of the sandy coves.

Golfo di Cognena—a deserted, rather flat and shallow bay with a good, well-sheltered anchorage at the mouth. Thick weed with patches of mud and sand in depths of 2 or 3 fathoms. No facilities of any kind.

Porto Rotondo is a charming small bay almost land-locked and hitherto frequented by smaller yachts. Unfortunately it has now come under the developer's influence, and already a small hotel and some villas have been set up. Nearly a dozen yachts (7- to 8-foot draught) can now be accommodated in the basin, berthing at a quay completed in 1968. Facilities such as fuel supply, water and provisions are likely to be laid on in the near future.

Golfo di Marinella. At the head of this gulf is a sandy beach overlooked by a modern luxury hotel. One may anchor 150 yards off the beach where in 3 fathoms the holding is good, and the anchorage exposed only to N.E. A small yacht may obtain better shelter in the small Novo Marinello cove where at the head of the creek inside the islet the bottom is sand with depths of 2 fathoms and less. Further out the bottom is rock and boulders.

On rounding the tall, massive Cape Figari and entering **Aranci Bay** one is struck by the dramatic mountain scenery and the greenness of the country-side. The anchorage has afforded shelter for ships of many navies since Nelson's day, and now its small fishing port has become the terminal for the fast car-ferry service with the Italian mainland.

Round the bay are some small coves with sandy beaches. Two of these are inaccessible by land and provide good shelter and agreeable anchorage for a yacht.

(a) Close N. of Tandy Islet.
(b) West of Isoletto Porri.

Golfo Aranci, a ferry-port in the centre of Aranci Bay which links Sardinia with Civitavecchia in eight hours (twice daily). The place is not recommended for yachts.

Approach. Chart 163, plan shows the approach.

Berth off the outer part of the western arm of the double quay.

Facilities. Fresh provisions can be bought, and the one hotel provides good meals and baths.

Olbia lies 3 miles up a narrow inlet in the heart of the granite mountains of Gallura; this commercial port, the third largest in Sardinia, has no attraction for a yacht.

Approach. Chart 3609. The channel marked by buoys leads in from Isola Bocca (with its conspicuous lighthouse) towards the steamer pier, 1 mile in length. A yacht should then pass through a narrow passage, clearly marked by buoys and beacons, leading to Molo Vecchio. By night it is difficult on account of the shallow patches which by day are evident because of the long stakes for mussel cultivation.

At the harbour entrance tidal streams are sometimes encountered.

Berth. West of the Molo Vecchio is a mole off which a yacht may berth with stern to the quay.

Officials. Yachts have sometimes had difficulty with the police who have insisted on pass-ports being handed in during the yacht's stay.

Facilities. Water is laid on to both the quay and the small yacht club (hose available). There are some good shops and an excellent market. There is a Jolly Hotel, one or two small ones, and some good restaurants. The railway runs from the port to Cagliari in six hours. A steamer runs regularly to Naples; other steamers, mostly freighters from Genoa, call irregularly.

Olbia, although a town of 20,000 people, has few attractions for the visitor today. It was founded by Phoenicians in the 4th century B.C.; afterwards Greek traders settled here on account of the Purple trade. Carthaginians, Romans, Pisans and Genoese, as well as Barbary pirates, all overran it in turn. The English fleet seized it during the reign of Queen Anne, afterwards handing it over to Austria. Only the Romans and Genoese have left architectural evidence, the one a necropolis and baths, the other the granite Romanesque cathedral of St. Simplicio, whose foundations date from the 4th century. Until recent years the population suffered from malaria, but by draining the marshes, and by the application of modern methods, this scourge has been completely eliminated. There are some good bathing beaches to seaward of Olbia inlet. Liscia Belle Saline on the southern side has a suitable anchorage for any size of yacht.

Golfo Aranci, the ferry-steamer terminus for Civitavecchia on the mainland, is 20 kilometres distant by road.

From the Gulf of Olbia the coast runs for a few miles in a S.E. direction as far as Coda Cavallo Point; it is well indented with off-lying, mountainous islands. The steep-to Tavolara Island (600 feet taller than Gibraltar) towers dramatically above the whole shore line, where a few interesting anchorages suitable for a yacht are tucked into bays on the green Sardinian shores.

Tavolara Island itself has a spit of sand jutting out to the S.W. on which stand a few ugly modern houses—the only possible place for dwellings by this

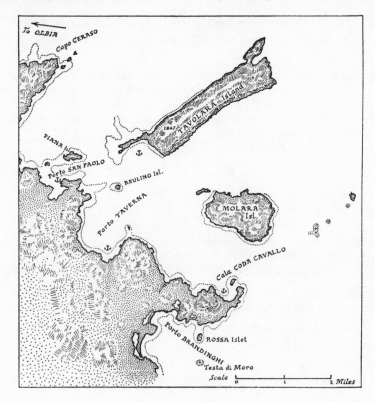

massive table mountain. The spit of sand forms a convenient anchorage, sheltered under normal conditions, where local craft bring up. Apart from the shelter there is nothing to make a visit worthwhile.

Porto San Paolo is suitable only for shallow draught yachts which can tuck inside the hook of land affording protection from the S.E. day breeze. There is nothing particularly attractive about this bay.

Porto Taverna. An open bay with anchorage at the S. corner in 3 fathoms. A large mooring buoy has been placed in the centre of this bay, and a number of villas are springing up above the shore.

The two coves of Cala Purgatorio and Sugaraccia lie about the middle of the bay and merit no description. Villas are also growing up here. At the eastern extremity of this stretch of coast is **Cala Coda Cavallo,** a charming unspoilt bay, with anchorage in convenient depths on a sandy bottom. 'Sheltered from all winds', say Sailing Directions. In 1967 the bay was completely deserted but a new road under construction following round the coast may herald the coming of future development. This place is well worth a visit.

Porto Brandinghi, southward of Cape Coda Cavallo, is given a detailed description in Sailing Directions. It has, however, no attraction for a yacht. being completely exposed to the day breeze and to south-easterly weather, Testa di Moro and other unmarked off-lying hazards prevent one from recommending Porto Brandinghi as a yacht anchorage.

The Coast now turns to the southward for over 100 miles to form the eastern seaboard of Sardinia. Although there are some minor anchorages, and nowadays a couple of artificial ports on this stretch of coast, the description recorded by Pausanius nearly two thousand years ago is still largely true—'An unbroken chain of impassable mountains, and if you sail along the coast you will find no anchorage on this side of the island, while violent but irregular gusts of wind sweep down to the sea from the tops of the mountains.'

La Caletta, a newly constructed timber-port, 6 miles N.W. of Cape Comino. It can be useful to a yacht on passage from one end of the island to the other.

Approach. Coming from the north one can see Posada village on the hill with its square, stone tower. The two breakwaters forming the harbour may be recognised, especially that extending in a S.E. direction from a point 100 yards W. of Torre di S. Giovanni.

Berth. Inside the entrance the depths diminish from 20 feet, but there is good holding, and excellent protection except from S.E.

Facilities. Two recently built, but modest, hotels, and some provision shops in the port. A type of beer made from rice is produced here.

Cala Gonone, a small port of call for coasters, is 18 miles S.W. of C. Comino. Its interest lies in the cave Del Bue Marino, sometimes inhabited by an almost extinct type of mammal, the monk seal.

Approach and Anchorages. In the mountains between Monte Tului (3,000 feet) W.N.W. of the cove and Dorgali village, is a conspicuous cleft easily discerned against the light-coloured mountains behind. It is then easy to make for the landing place. The cove is quite open and in settled weather one can anchor off in 2½ fathoms. [Photograph facing p. 48.]

The village of Dorgali, approached by road, lies 2¼ miles inland. The cave can be entered both by sea and by land, and the spring is the most likely time to see the monk seals.

Arbatax is a useful night anchorage for a yacht en route from one end of Sardinia to the other. It has a clean harbour enclosed in an attractive bay, but the adjoining village is of no particular interest.

Approach. Charts 161A and 1128, plan. Except in fresh N. to N.E. winds, it is easy to enter day or night, and Cape Bella Vista Lighthouse is an outstanding feature for many miles.

Berth off the northern quay with head towards west, but lay out an anchor to N.W., because strong land breezes are occasionally felt. The quay is a convenient height for landing from the yacht.

Facilities. There is no water on the quay, but the tap at the small boat dock nearby is accessible, and water may be fetched by dinghy. Limited fresh provisions can be bought at two local shops, but reasonable stocks are held at Tortoli, a village 3 miles distant. This may

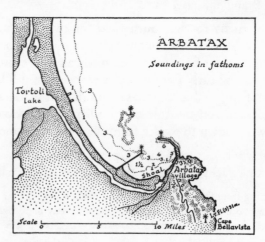

be reached by bus (not after 6.30 p.m.), or by taxi at a reasonable charge. At Tortoli, ice, fuel etc. are obtainable.

One small restaurant facing the harbour can provide meals. There are several bars. Good bathing from the breakwater or the beach.

A number of small coasters put in here mostly to load the products of the timber and plywood factory. In 1966 the Milanese manager was taken away by bandits and released only on payment of £16,000.

From Arbatax the coast turns south and runs for nearly 80 miles without a harbour until reaching the islet of Cavoli at the S.E. corner of Sardinia.

The winds off the coast continue to be variable most of the summer. Sudden changes in the direction of the gusts may be expected, especially during the very hot weather, when passing every little bay or valley; sometimes blowing strongly onshore, at others offshore with even greater strength. The occasional Sirocco gale, actuated by a depression, may also blow for a day, to be followed immediately by a fresh N. wind which adds to the confusion of the sea. With very hot unsettled weather many bush fires may sometimes be seen on the mountain slopes.

Close to the S.E. tip of Sardinia comes a more interesting stretch of coast with islands.

Some 5 miles N. of Cape Carbonara is a charming, but nameless, small sandy cove, facing south. Tucked under the green hilly slopes it is an ideal solitary anchorage for a yacht. Close to Cape Carbonara is:

Port Giunco, a broad and somewhat open anchorage sheltered from the N.W. wind blowing out of the Gulf of Cagliari. Off the long sandy beach small motor-boats sometimes moor here in summer, but the occasional Sirocco wind makes their position precarious and then they must either haul out on the beach or go to Carbonara. There is one modern hotel on the low ground by the beach, but otherwise the place is deserted.

Anchorage. Chart 3921. A suitable berth is close northward of Giunco Tower over a clear sandy bottom in depths of 3 to 4 fathoms.

Cape Carbonara, being at a windy corner of Sardinia, is of interest to a yacht because it provides a choice of anchorage, either one side or the other, completely sheltered from strong winds.

SOUTH COAST

The South Coast of Sardinia attracts very few sailing yachts, possibly because of its being rather a windy corner. There are, however, some interesting anchorages to be explored.

The large Gulf of Cagliari, with its mountainsides giving way to the plains behind them, and the city at its head, provides some pleasant sheltered anchorages. This is the fringe of a popular area where already new resorts have sprung up by the shores of each little sheltered bay.

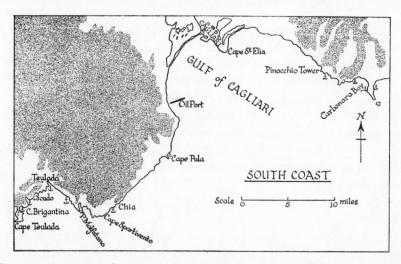

Carbonara Bay provides temporary anchorage in agreeable surroundings at the eastern arm of the gulf with unexpected good shelter from the prevailing W.N.W. wind.

> **Approach and Anchorage.** Chart 3921. By *day*, pass close eastward of Pescatelli Rocks (also avoiding the underwater Rock where the French lost two valuable storeships in 1793), and work northwards keeping 1 cable off the short projection of land with a new hotel. Anchor as convenient in 3 fathoms on one of the sandy patches. Shelter here is surprisingly good even though 500 yards out there may be a strong wind and rough sea. By *night* one must run in on the flashing light and anchor when reaching 3 to 5 fathoms, but in this case shelter from the prevailing wind may not be so good. This light has recently been reported as being unreliable.

The main road passes nearby and a summer hotel has recently been opened close above the shore.

There is also good shelter in a small sandy bay about 2 miles N.W. of Cape Boi, close eastward of **Pinocchio Tower**. This is more attractive than the spacious Carbonara Bay; some villas have recently grown up on its eastern slopes.

In event of shelter being needed from E. to N.E. winds a yacht should follow the example of the trawlers and anchor on the E. side of the bay, immediately N. of the ruined fort, yet S. of the protruding reef shown on the chart.

Cagliari. A large commercial port, capital of Sardinia, worthy of a visit.

Approach. Chart 1130, though 3921 is sufficient. The new extensions to the outer break-waters have improved the shelter within the port.

Berth. Secure at inner N.E. basin, among the Customs Craft, with anchor out and stern to the quay. This place has been cleaned up and is now under supervision of the port administration. The surroundings are pleasant.

Officials. Customs, Police and Harbour Master, all close at hand. There is no yacht club; only a few yachts visit the port. In the Harbour Office the Malta weather reports in English are available.

Facilities. Many shops for provisions are close by, and a market fifteen-minutes' walk to the westward. Some appetising meals at *trattorias* can be found in Via Cavour, the street immediately behind the esplanade. Hotels are nearby. Water by hydrant can be arranged through the Harbour Master. Ice from the factory in Vico Baroni Rossi. The local dry white wine can be bought, see page 71.

There are rail and bus services to the more interesting places in the island. Steamer service to Naples, Genoa and Messina. Air service to Rome and Naples. The modern port has expanded considerably and can now accommodate up to thirty steamers.

The city of about 200,000 inhabitants is of Phoenician origin. Today one sees the modern buildings and smart shops, all sprung up since the Second World War, but there are also two or three interesting medieval churches attributed to the Pisans, and architectural traces of four centuries of Spanish occupation. Something can be learnt of the original inhabitants by visiting the archaeological museum in the Piazza della Independenza, beside San Pancrazio Tower at the top of the old town within the bastions. Here is a remarkable collection of bronze sculpture and votive offerings of the Proto-Sard period (1400–1200 B.C.) before the first Carthaginian invasions. It is well worth a visit.

Continuing southwards, along the W. shore of the gulf, one comes to the oil port at **Sarroch.** This consists of an oil jetty, nearly a mile in length, with a large refinery by the shore. It is claimed to be well sheltered by the pier, but the place is now a military area.

Capo Pula lies on the point of a very small peninsula 10 miles N.W. of C. Spartivento. The anchorage in the bay immediately northwards provides a useful place for landing at the ruins of the ancient city of Nora. (See sketch plan overleaf.)

Approach. The prominent Aragonese watchtower on the headland is easily distinguished. On the N. side of the promontory is the anchorage and on the S. a shallow cove with a dyke for the fishery and for the protection of a few local boats. On the isthmus, sometimes to be seen from seaward, are the ruins of the ancient city.

Anchorage. One must avoid an area northward of the isthmus—weed and boulders—where part of the old city has become submerged for a distance of about 300 yards from the shore.

It is recommended to steer for St. Efesio church (a small building with a prominent belfry) on a westerly course and let go within about 300 yards of the shore where the depths are 3 to 4 fathoms and the sea-bed firm sand. Shelter from the day breeze (usually W. or S.) is good, but the anchorage is completely exposed to the eastward. Land in the dinghy on the beach close by the ruins.

Facilities. A substantial bar–restaurant for the campers is close by, but the village is a long walk.

Nora was of Phoenician and Carthaginian origin before coming under Roman rule when it continued as the principal trading city of Sardinia. It declined in the early centuries A.D. and was lost sight of until the recent excavations began in 1952. A burial-place, theatre, baths and mosaics have been uncovered; some pottery and sculpture of Punic an Roman origin has been taken to the National Museum at Cagliari. The site is well worth seeing.

Twelve kilometres distant and somewhat inland is the well-known Is Morus Hotel standing on the edge of the pinewoods.

During the Napoleonic Wars, Nelson's frigates often anchored at Pula, about half a mile offshore, to embark live sheep and bullocks.

The coast now continues straight southwards towards Cape Spartivento. The shore is wooded with pine trees and has many sandy beaches now accessible to campers. A small resort has sprung up at Santa Margherita. There are almost no indentations here where a yacht could conveniently bring up, except at either side of a small promontary with a tower called **Torre Chia.** The setting is charming, but the anchorage—3 fathoms on a sandy bottom—is entirely exposed to S.E.

At Cape Spartivento, where one might expect some change in the direction of the wind, it is an even bet whether the wind may be E. or W., especially during the summer months.

Port Malfatano, a deserted bay with good shelter from northern and westerly quadrants. The surrounding hills cause strong gusts to sweep down upon the anchorage, sometimes making it very uncomfortable; in S.E. winds it affords no shelter. Despite the hilly surroundings and inviting contours of the coast-line, this place lacks the appeal of other anchorages nearby.

Two miles N.W. of Cape Malfatano is **Torre Pirini** which guards a bay to the northward. The bay, sheltered from the S.E. through E. to N.W. provides anchorage off the beach in 5 fathoms. Closer inshore the bottom becomes rocky. The bay is quite deserted.

Port Teulada, a spacious sandy bay with a new harbour affording good shelter.

> **Approach.** Chart 3920 and plan on Chart 1128. Budello Tower N.E. of the port is conspicuous. There are no harbour lights.

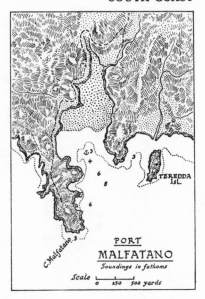

PORT
MALFATANO
Soundings in fathoms
Scale

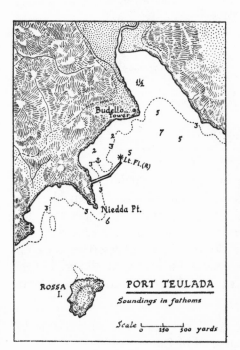

PORT TEULADA
Soundings in fathoms
Scale

Berth. One can anchor inside the breakwater with room to swing, or berth stern to the quay in depths of $2\frac{1}{2}$ fathoms; but the protecting wall has the effect of keeping out the breeze during hot weather.

Facilities. In 1967, water supplies were about to be laid on, but the only amenity then was a small bar.

The village of Teulada lies 4 miles inland. It has been known for the quality of the lace made by the inhabitants.

The long sandy beach and the attractive foothills with mountainous country behind have not yet attracted tourism. The port is usually empty and of no interest.

The two anchorages of Port Scudo and Cala Brigantina are open between S. and W.N.W., and though the holding at both places is good, most yachts would prefer the shelter of Port Teulada. From here after a short distance westward one comes to Cape Teulada—the western point of the south coast.

WEST COAST

The S.W. corner. Between Cape Teulada and San Pietro Island are some anchorages and the pleasant little port of Carloforte.

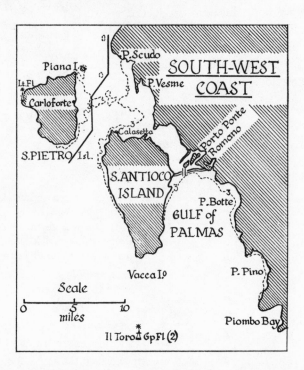

The Gulf of Palmas was much used in the sailing ship days because even in a southerly blow neither wind nor sea make this anchorage untenable. 'The finest open road-stead I have ever seen', wrote Nelson in December 1803. For small vessels wanting shelter from winds in the easterly quadrant there is a choice of **Piombo Bay, Porto Pino** and **Porto Botte,** all described in Sailing Directions, as well as other places with good holding towards the head of the bay. If desiring complete shelter there is the small artificial coaling port Ponte Romano at the N.W. corner of the Bay.

Porto Ponte Romano, an unattractive small coaling port which can be useful to a yacht in event of bad weather in the Gulf of Palmas.

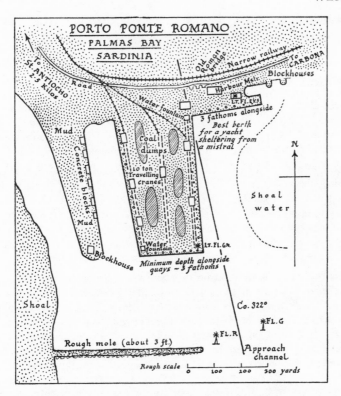

Approach. Chart 3915, plan. A line of buoys follows the channel into the port, maintaining approximately 3½ fathom depths in the dredged canal. A canal also leads through to San Antiocco.

Berth. The plan shows that most of the quays are allocated for the use of small freighters with depths of 3 fathoms alongside. The most convenient berth for a yacht is probably alongside the northern quay, but almost everywhere is subject to coal dust.

Officials. Customs, Harbour Master and Police have their offices near the northern quay.

Facilities. Fresh water is available at a fountain by the north quay, also very limited fresh food supplies and a restaurant.

Sant' Antioco, formerly an island, lies on the road beyond the Roman bridge, and nearby is the modern mining town of Carbonia (15,000 people) built during Mussolini's time. This is only 2 or 3 kilometres from the port, and here fresh provisions are easily obtainable. Beyond Sant' Antioco comes Fortuna Hill with its many Roman tombs and acropolis. Calasetta, the small ferry-port for the short crossing to Carloforte (on San Pietro Island) lies at the N.W. point of Sant' Antioco.

Both a road and a narrow-gauge railway lead from Calasetta in an easterly direction towards Cagliari, a two-hour journey by train.

Carloforte, the fishing port on San Pietro Island is sheltered, attractive, and makes an agreeable port of call.

Approach. Chart 3915, plan, shows the approach through the clear, shallow water over a sandy bottom. The buoys are not always in accordance with the chart; an additional one has been laid to mark the seaward end of the approach channel (i.e. about 2 cables west of Secca del Marini). The leading marks for both channels are conspicuous.

Berth south of the steamer quay (in the centre), but the holding on soft mud is poor. With a S.E. wind, shelter within the harbour is insufficient and it is advisable to anchor in the southern part, where conditions are better and the water cleaner; but it is further to row in the dinghy to reach the quay. A small yacht may also berth off the steamer quay, bearing in mind that the depths shoal to 4 feet within 10 feet of the quay.

A strong Mistral piles up the water in the strait, raising the sea level and reflecting waves into Carloforte harbour which cause flooding of the quays and streets.

Facilities. Fresh water from reservoirs may be obtained from a tap on the steamer quay (not between the hours of 13.00 and 17.00). One of the ferry steamers may sometimes lend a hose. Ice may be bought from one of the fish storage sheds at the southern end of the quays. A morning market for fish and meat; vegetable and fruit shops are good. A new first class hotel and simple but good restaurants close by. Local wine comes from Calasetta and is somewhat acid. Ferry steamers run to the two mainland ports across the strait—to Port Vesme with rail and bus connections to Cagliari, and to the small port of Calasetta.

In the port a number of *tartanes* lie at permanent moorings. Under lateen sail and jib they used to collect both salt and minerals which were delivered alongside the waiting steamers, a task that is now undertaken by lorry and barge.

The inhabitants of San Pietro Island are mostly occupied with tunny fishing, and some work at the canning factory; others, in recent years, have devoted their interests towards furthering the small, but growing tourist trade. The historical background of these island people is very different from the rest of the Sardinians. Coming from North Africa, two hundred years ago, they are descendants of a Genoese colony established at Tabarca in the Middle Ages. In consequence of their uncertain future at the mercy of a hostile Arab population, an expedition was organized in 1737 during the reign of Carlo Emmanuele of Savoy to bring them off to the safety of Sardinia. They were settled in the island of San Pietro. A statue to this benevolent monarch stands in the small square by the port; but it may be noticed that a hand is missing: this occurred when the statue was damaged during civil disturbances at the time of the French revolution.

Carloforte is a fascinating little town, and the people, despite some poverty, are well turned out and amiable to visitors. Their language is neither Genoese nor yet the same as other dialects spoken on the main island of Sardinia. From the port a line of palms follows the quayside as far as the *Capitaneria*, and thence the quay leads on to the *Tonara* where tunny are landed and cut up for canning. The little Port Vesme on the opposite shore also takes part in this industry. Two or three modest hotels take summer visitors, and recently a more modern one has been opened on the waterfront. Of the restaurants, one or two by the port serve excellent fish, the soft-shell lobster and tunny roes are local specialities.

Although the island is relatively flat a pleasant excursion may be made by bus from Carloforte passing through some unspoilt villages and thence following the coast to a sandy bay with a good bathing beach. Near the town the shores are rocky and uninviting for bathing.

When Nelson's flagship, *Vanguard*, entered these sheltered waters shortly before the Battle of the Nile, she was almost a wreck. During a severe Mistral in the Gulf of Lions she had been dismasted and only by good seamanship and good fortune was she towed into the safety of Carloforte. She had lost her foremast, foretopmast, top gallant and all yards forward, her bowsprit was sprung, main topmast, top gallant mast and all yards (except top gallant yard) were lost, mizzen topmast, top gallant mast and all yards belonging thereto were also lost. With help from other ships they re-rigged her in four days—'and if the ship had been in England, months would have been taken to send her to sea', wrote Nelson to his wife. But he deplored the fact that the ship's company were not permitted to land; 'we are refused the rights of humanity', he added. Crews of all belligerent ships were forbidden to go ashore because at this stage of the war Sardinia had recently proclaimed her neutrality.

The coast from Carloforte northwards towards Alghero is dull with uninviting cliffs. The best shelter is halfway along at the anchorage of Oristano.

Oristano. Conveniently situated in isolated surroundings, this large gulf is especially useful as a night anchorage when sailing from one end of the island to the other.

Approach. Chart 3917. When coming from the south there are no dangers, but approaching from N. one should have in mind Mal di Ventre Island with the outlying shoals.

Anchorage. A yacht may anchor on sand in convenient depths.
  (a) In the N.E. corner of the bay;
  (b) on the W. side of the bay, close N. of Cape S. Marco, in a sandy cove overlooked by a large round tower.

93

Facilities. At the N.E. corner of the bay one may land at the quay and get a taxi to Oristano village where provisions can be bought. There is also a café by the quay.

If landing on the W. side it is necessary to walk across to the modern hamlet of San Giovanni where fresh provisions can be bought.

Some Phoenician ruins lie under water near the above-mentioned anchorage at S. Giovanni di Sinis. If one walks to the village of Cabras a local wine, called *Vernaccia*, can be bought from the bottlers; but having a proof strength of 20° it should be treated with respect. The Tirso River (93 miles in length) flows into the Gulf of Oristano 5 miles E.N.E. of C. San Marco, but although the longest river in Sardinia, it is unnavigable. Trout are fished in the upper reaches.

If the wind should be south of west one may equally well anchor under the lee of Cape Frasca, where apart from the small fishing craft the place is largely deserted.

Bosa Marina. A river mouth and a partially sheltered bay lying in attractive scenery.

Approach. Chart 161B, and there is also a plan on Italian Chart 287, which is more useful if entering the River Temo. This is the only Sardinian river with a navigable stretch—about 5 miles upstream from the river mouth. Here the entrance is narrow and it is unwise for a deep draught yacht to enter with an onshore wind. The channel, which has 7- to 8-foot depths, should be followed, and a yacht not exceeding 6-foot draught can proceed as far as Bosa.

If a night anchorage is needed without entering the river there is a suitable cove eastward of Rossa Islet. (See *M. & P.*)

Berth. (a) In the river alongside the quay on the S. side or with stern to the quay at the east end, or (b) in the bay at the E. of the island on the north side of the quay (11 feet alongside). Care should be taken to avoid small boat moorings on the N. side.

The bay, open only to winds between S. and W., is suitable as an anchorage and is well-sheltered against winds from other directions.

Facilities. The small town of 8,000 inhabitants is some distance away and the amenities nearby are very limited. A local red wine can be bought.

Despite some hideous buildings, the general setting is attractive, and the new harbour works are an indication of a growing prosperity.

Alghero, a pleasant medieval walled town of Catalan origin, recently became Sardinia's principal tourist resort.

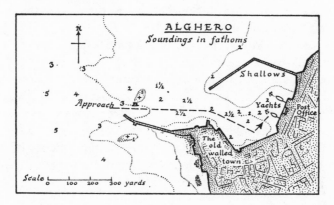

Approach. Chart 1128 with plan. The approach inside the southern breakwater has been dredged and the Banchina Doganale deepened.

Berth at the Banchina Doganale, with anchor laid to N.W., stern to the quay; but the holding is poor. [Photograph facing p. 48.]

Officials. The new Port Office has been built by the quay further to the N.E.

Facilities. Water is laid on to the quay and may be obtained by permit from the municipal building nearby. A good and cheap market for fish, vegetables and fruit is in the centre of the town. Ice factory is in a corner at the right-angle of the two quays. Petrol and diesel fuel obtainable from Esso garage, but an issue of duty-free fuel is made only in large quantities. Several hotels and restaurants in the modern residential part of the town to the S.E. and one or two small restaurants serving a good fish course close by. The airport with connection to Milan, Rome and sometimes London, is 11 kilometers from the town; there is also an efficient and cheap air service to Cagliari.

Alghero, a town of 28,000 people, still has its medieval Spanish atmosphere, with the old walls surrounding dilapidated houses; washing is hung across narrow cobbled streets, and in the small port fishermen still speak Catalan. Here one sees the small coasters busily loading exports of lime, cork and fish from the quays. On both sides of the old town new suburbs are growing up, one for the local merchants and residents, the other on the sea front as the tourist resort. Except for the old part the place seems to be flourishing, and the few well-built villas one sees in the background, were formerly owned by well-to-do refugees from central European states who had fled here after the First World War.

The cool sea breeze sets in from N.W. to S.W. during the afternoon. Tourists drive to the sandy bathing beaches north of the town, where, before the First World War, Grand Admiral von Tirpitz owned a large estate.

There are bus services to other Sardinian towns, including Sassari, the provincial capital. Continuing along this route one can reach Corsica within the day: the bus follows the road to Sta. Teresa and there one catches the ferry across the Bonifacio Strait to the port of Bonifacio.

Cape Caccia is well known for the underwater fishing, and nearby is the famous Nettuno Grotto, mentioned more than a century ago by Admiral Smyth who, in 1824, placed Bengal Lights at its entrance. It is now electrically lit and can be reached either by a tourist motor-boat or by Auto–Pullman. If one leaves the road, by a turning to the right, after passing Cantoniera de Pera bridge, one reaches a restored *nuraghi*. From the bronze objects found inside it has been dated about 750 B.C.—a period of commercial prosperity when *nuraghe* increased both in size and in their defensive nature. Bearing away to the left one comes to the Bombard Beach and a modern hotel.

Porto Conte, a large and partially land-locked bay, convenient for a night's anchorage. The area is now being developed as a summer resort.

Approach. Chart 1128. There is no difficulty. Cape Caccia Lighthouse on the western end of entrance makes a good mark.

Anchorages. Anchor in one of the coves according to the weather.
(a) In Cala del Bollo, which has a prominent new hotel on the ridge south of the tower, there is anchorage on thick weed with occasional patches of sand or gravel. Open to the southerly swell.
(b) N.E. of Torre Nicova is an anchorage by some new hotels, where the shelter is probably better.

The afternoon day breeze is N.W. and puffs from the mountains can stir up a short sea inside the bay.

Swordfish boats in the Messina Strait, the old and the new

The fishing village of Porticello, Sicily

The medieval fishing port of Cefalù

The Greek theatre at Taormina

Facilities. The village is small with limited facilities. There are large hotels at both the above anchorages.

On the northern shore is a popular bathing beach, visited by tourists from Alghero. A new coastal road follows round the bay towards Cape Caccia, and during summer there is a stream of cars bringing visitors to enjoy the view from this tall headland.

From Cape Caccia northwards the coast is steep-to and rocky for 25 miles until one comes to Asinara Island with the entrance to the Fornelli Passage.

Fornelli Passage. This 10-foot passage between Asinara Island and the Sardinian coast affords a useful short-cut. Neither the chart nor Sailing Directions indicate the leading-marks which are sited on the rocky southern shore of Asinara Island. The minimum depth (10 feet) is near the small islet about mid-

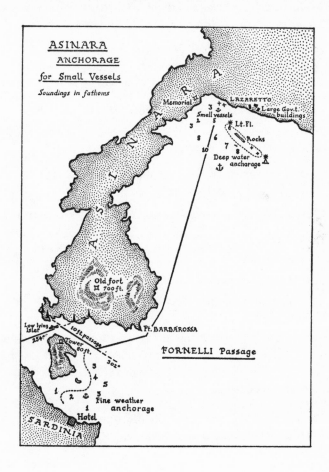

way through the channel, where there are sometimes tidal streams which occasionally run at nearly 2 knots.

Approach. Chart 3916. The old fort on the hill of Monte Castellaccio (700 feet) is conspicuous from seaward, and during the approach also the tower on Piana Island. The three lattice towers support high-tension cables between Piana Island and Asinara. They have a least height above water of 85 feet. The masonry leading marks should be brought into transit on about 074°, and after passing the low-lying rock to port the two marks on the S.W. of Asinara Island will be brought into transit when bearing about 302°. Course should then be altered to the reciprocal of this bearing and the line of transit maintained until reaching deeper water. The bottom is mostly sand.

Anchorage. In fine weather one may anchor E.S.E. of Piana Island in convenient depths on a sandy bottom, but one must remember that many small fishing craft are under way at night. A large tourist hotel has recently grown up on the Sardinian shore.

The Island of Asinara has been a convict settlement for many decades, and one can see the government buildings in the elbow bend off which small vessels can anchor.

Anchorage. The best anchorage is close westward of the rocky islet in the N. corner of the bay (Rada della Reale). The depths are from 5 to 6 fathoms on a bottom of weed on sand. Further inshore there is usually better shelter, but the bottom is rocky and irregular. A number of underwater rocks extend from the northern shore towards the east.

Facilities. Although a landing can be made at a pier near the quarantine building, there are no facilities and it is normally prohibited.

Port Torres. A large, artificial, commercial port. Although it affords complete shelter, it is of no interest to a yacht.

Approach. Plan on Chart 1128. The western mole has recently been extended seawards.

Berth in the Darsena or eastern part of the harbour, entered through a narrow passage from the outer harbour. (Do not berth in the inner harbour.) Yachts berth with anchor to N. and stern to S. quay, where there is now over 2 fathoms depth, but the place can be smelly.

Officials. Capitaneria is a few yards from the berth.

Facilities. There are adequate shops for provisions, but there is no water laid on. Shell and Esso have fuel depots in the port.

The town, with about 12,000 inhabitants, is unattractive, but it serves as the port for Sassari, capital of the northern province. A yacht should regard the port only as a useful place for shelter. The Genoa steamer calls daily in summer and there is a service to Corsica.

Castel Sardo, an attractive old town on the hill with fine cathedral worth visiting; but shelter for a yacht is somewhat lacking.

Approach and Berth. Chart 3916. The cathedral tower on the hillside is conspicuous, and seen from westward, resembles a lighthouse. A shallow harbour has been formed by joining the islet to the western shore of the small cove to the westward of the town. You approach by leaving the islet to starboard and following the channel towards a quay. For a yacht drawing more than 5 feet it is advisable to anchor in the cove close beside the citadel, and land in the dinghy, but it is somewhat exposed to the day breeze.

Facilities. Provisions are scarce. A restaurant above the waterfront serves a palatable meal.

The attractive old town of 4,000 people was founded as a Roman colony. It stands on the hill and is approached by narrow streets ascending to the fine Pisan cathedral of San Goveno; built by Lombardy architects in the 11th century it is remarkable for the Doric and Corinthian columns supporting the roof.

The inhabitants are mostly occupied with fishing, and in making carpets and baskets. Many lobsters are caught here and flown to Marseilles.

Twenty-eight miles to the N.E. is Cape Testa (conspicuous for its lighthouse and white sand), the S.W. entrance to Bonifacio Strait. With offshore winds a useful anchorage en route is behind Rossa Island.

SICILY AND ADJACENT ISLANDS

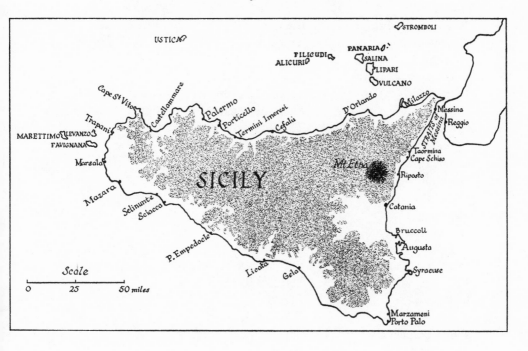

STRAIT OF MESSINA
Messina
Reggio (Calabria)
Taormina
Mazzaro Bay
Porto di Sant' Andrea
Cape Schiso

EAST COAST
Riposto
Catania
Bruccoli
Porto di Augusta
Syracuse
Marzameni

SOUTH COAST
Porto Palo
Gela
Licata
Porto Empedocle
(*Agrigento*)
Sciacca
(*Selinunte*)
Mazara del Vallo

WEST COAST
Marsala
Island of Pantelleria
Trapani

AEGADEAN ISLANDS
Island of Favignana
Island of Levanzo
The Formiche Islets
Island of Marettimo

NORTH COAST
Island of Ustica
San Vito
Castellammare del Golfo
Palermo
Porticello
Termini Imeresi
Cefalù
Cape D'Orlando
Cape Milazzo Anchorage
Milazzo

LIPARI OR AEOLIAN ISLANDS
Island and
Port of Lipari
Island of Vulcano
Island of Salina
Island of Panaria
Island of Stromboli

5

Sicily and Adjacent Islands

Although Sicily is only slightly larger than Sardinia, its population is more than three times as great. In appearance the tall mountains with wooded foot-hills somewhat resemble those of Calabria, but Sicily boasts a volcano (Mt. Etna 10,742 feet) still intermittently in a state of eruption. Despite the absence of rivers and the dried-up appearance of the land all the summer months, it is claimed that 90 per cent of Sicily is cultivated.

On the south coast and part of the north are the fruit trees: almonds, olives, lemons and orange groves; from the foot of Mt. Etna extends the great central plain where the corn is grown—the granary of Italy in Roman days. Very little wild life is to be seen—a few foxes, wildcats, martens, boars and rabbits; most of the birds are migratory, hardly a sparrow residing in the island.

Since the days of Homer, Sicily has been a focal point of history and the number of splendid architectural monuments still surviving make it one of the most interesting places to visit. The island has been overrun by almost every power: beginning with the Phoenicians and followed in succession by Carthaginians, Greeks, Romans and Saracens. But not until it was seized early in the 11th century by Norman adventurers were churches and palaces built, worthy to stand beside the temples of the great Greek period. After the Normans the government of the island was in dispute, and unhappily the Pope allowed Charles of Anjou to keep the Kingdom of the Two Sicilies; unpopu-larity and misgovernment resulted in the well-known Sicilian Vespers: this began on Easter Day 1282 when a Frenchman insulted a Sicilian woman outside a church and in the ensuing riot about 8,000 French were killed.

Later the British administered the island for nine years. After the historic campaign of Garibaldi the last assault on the island was in 1943 when an Allied force of 160,000 men landed on the southern beaches and drove out the German invaders, most of whom escaped across the Messina Strait to the mainland. In our times Sicily has been in the news either when the activities of the Mafia have become notorious or when there is an earthquake.

After such a disturbed and eventful history it is not surprising to find the people different from those elsewhere in Italy. Their language is a form of Italian with Greek and Arabic expressions; a few Norman and Spanish words have crept in. Many Sicilians bear the unmistakable features of Arab ancestry and a number of places have Arab names.

The present population of nearly five million is well distributed among the country villages and the large towns of Palermo, Catania and Messina, which, despite a certain amount of squalor, are very slowly becoming modernized. In the country there has been very limited improvement in the economy although the government, based on constitutional legislation in Rome, enjoys a wider form of autonomy than other states, except Sardinia. Sicily sends to Italy very large shipments of lemons, oranges and almonds; lesser quantities of sulphur, grain and fish, and very recently cargoes of oil. Nevertheless, the unfortunate peasants, fishermen and miners, still have a low standard of living; a considerable percentage are unemployed and the rest suffer from absentee landlords.

Ancient Monuments. Many fine buildings dating from the Hellenic period to the end of the Middle Ages still remain in a good state of preservation. Foremost among them all are the Greek temples at Selinunte and Segesta; and the theatres at Taormina, Tyndari, Palazzolo, Catania and Syracuse.

The Normans left behind splendid churches at Palermo, Monreale and Cefalù; these are Romanesque in conception decorated with mosaics carried out by Greek craftsmen. Guide-books should be consulted for details of these buildings. There is practically no Gothic architecture in Sicily, the pointed arches which in some ways resemble it being of Arab origin.

Food and Wine. In the larger towns, especially those visited by tourists, such as Taormina, Palermo and Syracuse, there are some excellent restaurants well up to mainland standards. Elsewhere food can be disappointing with a preponderance of local dishes with too much olive oil.

Sicilian wines, originally cultivated by the Greeks, which were so famous in Roman times, can no longer claim to maintain that high standard. Most people have heard of the fortified Marsala wines once popular as a dessert wine in England. Sicilian wines today are often coarse and heavy, although a few palatable table wines can be found, near Syracuse and Palermo, and especially at Casteldaccia. The wines from grapes grown in the extensive Etna vineyards—a white wine and a rosé, sometimes slightly fizzy, are sold everywhere —'58 and '61 were good years. *Lipari* wines from the Aeolian Islands and Milazzo are slightly sweet—'52 and '60 were said to be good years. *Mamertino* is similar. There is *Faro* a reasonably dry red wine from the vicinity of Messina.

But most of Sicily's vineyards are owned by the great wine concerns which so far have failed to improve the quality of the vines as has been done in Sardinia.

Ports and Anchorages. Although there is so much interest ashore, few of Sicily's thirty ports and anchorages can be called entirely suitable for a yacht. Places are set out in a clockwise direction, beginning with the Messina Strait.

THE STRAIT OF MESSINA

Far on the right her dogs foul Scylla hides,
Charybdis roaring on the left presides,
And in her greedy whirlpool sucks the tides,
Then spouts from them below, with fury driven,
The waves mount up, and wash the face of Heaven,
But Scylla from her den, with open jaws,
The sinking vessel in her eddy draws,
Then dashes on the rocks.

VIRGIL, *The Aeneid*, III, trans. Dryden

A sailing yacht wishing to pass through the Messina Strait should arrange to do so with a favourable tidal stream. She should also shape a course to avoid the three permanent whirlpools marked on the chart; one south of Punto San

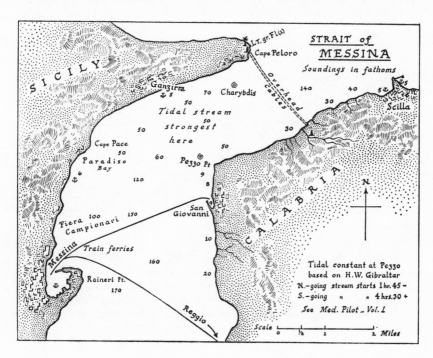

Raineri, Charybdis, and the third close off Punta Pezzo. Yachts should also be careful to avoid the train ferries which demand right of way with regard to a small yacht, and lastly a sailing yacht should, if possible, avoid making this passage in unsettled weather when unpredictable squalls are apt to blow with great strength from the steep mountain valleys. Use of the engine is invariably the best course.

Tidal streams and currents. According to Sailing Directions the waters of the Ionian Sea (southward) are appreciably colder and more salt than those of the Tyrrhenian Sea (northward). The difference in density of the waters at the two ends of the strait sets up currents which flow southward through the strait on the surface and northward below a depth of about 10 fathoms. In early times, we find Thucydides making the observation 'that where Sicily is the least distance from the Continent this is the so called Charybdis through which Odysseus is said to have sailed. It has naturally become accounted dangerous because of the narrowness, and of the currents caused by the inrush of the Tyrrhenian Sea.' As this south-going current flows at a rate of only about ¼ knot (unless stopped by a north wind), it need not be considered in our calculations; but tidal streams running for six and a quarter hours each way at considerable strength (springs 4½ knots, neaps 2½) should be studied before making this passage. The change in direction of these streams is easily calculated by applying the Tidal Constant (quoted in Sailing Directions) to the time of H.W. at Gibraltar. At the turn of the tide, there is a brief stand of no movement and then with the new tide setting in comes a line of 'bores' known as *tagli*—short waves whose crests lie across the strait. Under normal conditions they are not dangerous, and only with a fresh wind blowing against an advancing *taglio* (especially the 'Second *Taglio*' off Punta Pezzo), is a small vessel likely to be endangered. But at night when one may sometimes hear, but not see, the advancing *tagli*, one awaits the approaching waves with trepidation.

Whirlpools and eddies. The main whirlpools have been mentioned. They are indicated by huge, smooth, revolving, oily patches, where the denser water is sinking and the other water is welling up from below. They occur over unusual irregular formations on the bottom; no whirlpools operate constantly. They come and go, then boil up close by; there are a number of less significant whirlpools, as well as eddies close under headlands inshore where little counter-currents set in.

One may wonder why Scilla, so formidable to the ancients, has not been mentioned. In 1783 a violent earthquake so changed the local topography that Scilla is now barely perceptible, and no longer would Ulysses complain at finding himself back 'at the rocks of Scilla and the terrifying whirlpool'; Charybdis also is less impressive now than it was in the early centuries.

Train-ferry ports. Ferries run from the two mainland ports of San Giovanni and Reggio across to the Sicilian terminal at Messina. Except for San Giovanni which has no other accommodation, the two ports of Reggio and Messina, described later in detail, are both unsuitable for a yacht. When under way one should be careful to keep well clear of these ferries which carry trains continuously across the strait—day and night. Nowadays passengers to and from Sicily (Reggio to Messina) cross by hydrofoil ferry which causes a disturbing wash inside the ports.

106

Winds. In unsettled weather squalls may rush down the deep valleys and strike the sea often in an unexpected direction. One hesitates to enlarge upon the description in St. John III, v. 8: 'The wind bloweth where it listeth, and thou hearest the sound thereof, but canst not tell whence it cometh and whither it goeth.'

Normally, during early summer a good proportion of southerly winds can be expected, but in July, August and early September winds are usually in the northern quadrant.

Entering the Strait. Having ascertained from Sailing Directions the most favourable time to pass through and noted the timing of the counter-currents, one can then decide whether to follow the Sicilian or the Calabrian coast. By day and in fine weather it is more interesting to hug the Sicilian shores passing within a cable of the beach most of the way. Each village of small fishermen's houses spreads itself along the shore overlapping its neighbour; one may sometimes see great activity among the local fishing craft, especially among the swordfish boats at Ganzirra.

On a clear night the brightly lit shores with endless lines of lights and the hill villages twinkling, as though with fairy lamps, give one a feeling of passing along a great illuminated highway. The old sailing ships found it very different, for they complained of being dazzled by the fishermen's torches which prevented their seeing the poor harbour lights of Messina.

Anchorage. In the event of a medium-sized yacht seeking a night anchorage, either before entering or on leaving Messina Strait, the small harbour of Scilla is probably as good as any. Inside the Strait are the unsuitable ferry ports of Messina and Reggio as well as three anchorages off the Sicilian shore—Ganzirra, Paradiso Bay, Fiera Campionari—all referred to in Sailing Directions, where in fine weather, one may anchor with reasonable comfort. Of the three, Paradiso, a sandy bay overlooked by the former palace of the governor, is certainly the most pleasant for a yacht. The only anchorage used by local craft is Fiera Campionari; nearly all haul out and even the large swordfish boats are hauled up on the beach.

At Cape Peloro, which is flat, a very tall pylon (764 feet) supports the Sicilian end of the 2-mile span of power cables reaching across to the high Calabrian coast. A modern lighthouse has replaced the fortified light tower, which only a hundred years ago was protected by two batteries, two Martello towers and covered by a strongpoint called 'Telegraph Redoubt'. On the north side the fine sandy beach has become a bathing resort with large hotels, but on the south side the beach is steep-to.

It was off here that the old sailing ships used to anchor to embark their pilots for the Strait. Garibaldi found this beach useful for embarking his troops on 19th August, 1860, in order to cross the Strait to attack Reggio and other Calabrian objectives, and had little difficulty in evading enemy warships which were attempting to prevent his passage. A similar situation occurred in August

1943 when, in the face of only weak naval opposition, the retreating German army in Sicily also successfully escaped across the Messina Strait. In this case modern landing craft were used and men were embarked not only from Faro but also from the beaches at Ganzirra and Paradiso (already mentioned as being anchorages). Their Italian allies, being less hurried, chose the more comfortable train-ferries. Altogether within approximately ten days an army of 100,000 men was ferried across, taking with them 100 guns and 10,000 vehicles.

Swordfish in the Strait of Messina. These valuable fish swim southwards during the spring and north (and westwards) about June; this later period is when the Messina fishermen hunt them in special four-oared boats with a substantial mast for the look-out in the middle. The harpooner uses a 9-foot weapon and the captain from the masthead gives all orders. The fish, weighing from 4 to 500 kilograms are usually sold at 500 lire per kilo. A new type of boat with a lattice steel mast and long bowsprit has now been introduced—see photograph facing page 96.

Swordfishermen off Scilla

Messina. This modern port, serving a city of more than a quarter of a million people, is Sicily's main link with Italy. The strong tides within the harbour and the busy ferry-steamers make it a disturbing place for a yacht to berth.

Approach. Chart 177. Although there is no difficulty it is prudent to study the tides described in Sailing Directions.

Berth. Deep water continues right up to the quays, which project rather dangerously under water; it is therefore difficult to find an agreeable place to berth. The strong tidal stream and the ferry wash add to the discomfort. (The first three hours of the *scendente* are when the harbour current runs at its strongest.)

This large modern city spreads itself for nearly 3 miles along the shores of the Strait at the foot of Mt. Peloritano, and despite the severe earthquake of 1908 which wrecked the entire town, its population has again increased, making it the third largest city of Sicily. When the earthquake occurred, the shores of Messina subsided two feet and shocks continued for two months; 84,000 people died, and many more in the neighbourhood were drowned due to the subsequent tidal wave. The next disaster was during the Second World War when the town, occupied by Germans, was bombarded by the Allies, and 5,000 Italians were killed. Since then the Norman cathedral and the church of the Annunziata have been rebuilt; and, although it is hardly surprising that skyscrapers have not been encouraged, the city now has a modern and presentable appearance.

Reggio. The town has become a Calabrian summer resort with a fine view of the Sicilian mountains across the Strait. The port, which is quite apart, handles the train-ferry traffic and, although there are almost no facilities a yacht can berth, though somewhat inconveniently, at the long wharf.

Approach. Chart 177. Not difficult day or night.

Berth. The only place to lie is south of the quay in the N.E. corner of the harbour. Although the holding here is good the place is usually dirty with much oil floating around. Yachts should never lie alongside on account of the disturbing wash from the hydrofoil ferry.

Officials. The Post Office with Customs and Police in the same building is very near.

Facilities. Fuel and water on the quay. Provisions in the town—fifteen minutes' walk. Train to Rome in nine hours—hydrofoil to Messina—air connections to Rome, Syracuse and other towns.

Reggio, originally colonized by Euboean Greeks and in Roman times known as Rhegium, has also been unfortunate in suffering from earthquake destruction. In 1783 and again in 1908 it was completely destroyed with much loss of life.

The present town of 150,000 inhabitants was rebuilt on the same site but planned with only two-storey houses, which has caused it to be far more spread out. It has now grown considerably, having become a modern resort well laid out with trees and gardens.

When Edward Lear was painting here in the middle of the last century he wrote, 'all the fullness of Sicilian vegetation awaits you. In the foreground, almonds, olives, cactus, palm trees, aloes and figs forming a delightful combination wherever you turn your steps.' At the same time, other visitors to Reggio were writing descriptions of the *Fata Morgana*, a phenomenon under the legendary influence of the Queen of the Fairies. This occurs in the Messina

Strait during warm weather, when tides are at their highest. It is similar to a mirage when, due to layers of air of different refractive value, shore objects, much elongated, appear above the horizon. They stand out very clearly and make a great impression on an observer who can view them to best advantage from Reggio. Similar phenomena are known to occur in African deserts and on the Hungarian plains.

Returning to the Sicilian shores, you come to **Taormina,** a small and ancient town which, despite its popularity among tourists, still holds great attraction. It stands high upon the hillside, overlooking both Mount Etna and the Strait of Messina. The nearest accessible port for a yacht is either Cape Schiso or the cove of Mazzaro. Unfortunately, neither are safe places to leave a yacht unattended. Yachts occasionally anchor on the rocky bottom at Porto S. Andrea between Cape St. Andrew and Isola Bella, but this is somewhat remote. Both from Cape Schiso and from Mazzaro one can reach Taormina by a short bus ride, zigzagging up the steep slopes of the mountainside. In the event of bad weather from any direction other than north, Riposto (see page 112) is the best place to make for.

On reaching Taormina one usually finds its winding streets and small attractive shops filled with visitors. One should, however, climb further up the hill or walk out to the Greek ruins to enjoy the view. (Photograph facing page 49.) Writers of the Victorian era were enraptured by the romantic nature of Sicilian scenery. The view was described a century ago: 'The ruins of the Greek theatre with the sea of amethyst seen through its broken arches might suffice of itself; but there comes Aetna beyond, displaying its magnificent flank and sweeping down to the ocean. Bits of the town, an old fortress above, a sugarloaf village beyond with various heights and peaks fill up the scene which is rendered doubly enchanting by the atmosphere and the sun which reveal it so distinctly and so brilliantly.'

A sailing-yacht will seldom enjoy cruising down the east coast of Sicily. It is too often bedevilled with gusts of wind off the mountains, while their aftermath is a short bumpy sea.

Mazzaro Bay, a charming but insecure cove convenient for a short stay off Taormina.

Approach. See plan above and chart 3935. It is easy by day, but nearly impossible by night. Coming from the east a yacht should pass between the Scoglio Mazzaro (20 feet) and the high coast opposite, thence round the southern headland and into the cove.

Anchorage. Steer for the prominent rock (12 feet) close to the sandy beach, and let go in 5 fathoms as in plan, and take a stern warp to the top of the rock. The bottom is rocky with

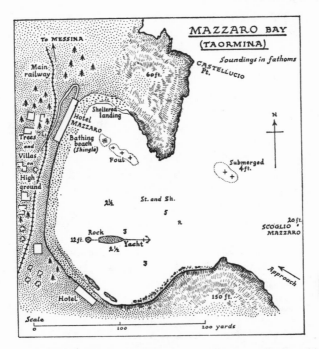

patches of shingle and large stones, and since there is often a swell, the cable is apt to be hooked under one of these obstructions and cause hard snubs on the cable holder. Even in fine weather this anchorage can be uncomfortable.

Facilities. It is usually most sheltered for landing in a dinghy in the N. corner of the cove behind a rock awash. The road which leads up from the bay joins a main road with bus communication to Taormina on the hill above. One can also reach it by footpath in half an hour. A general store is on the road nearby, and also the pleasant Hotel Mazzaro. The beach which mostly shingle, is usually thronged with bathers, many from Taormina.

Porto di Sant' Andrea, lying south of the small peninsula, also provides a useful anchorage when visiting Taormina. Some yachts which have experienced the uncomfortable swell in Mazzaro Bay prefer this place instead. The depths are shallow, but one may run out a warp to the rocks and land in the dinghy at the foot of some steps.

Cape Schiso. Behind the cape a short mole has recently been built to provide reasonable shelter against the N.E. wind. Two or three yachts can lie here temporarily while a visit is made to Taormina.

Approach and Anchorage. Make for the southern end of Taormina Roads (Chart 180). After rounding the extremity of the mole, anchor close to the quay, at the same time taking a warp to a bollard. (The mole extends only about 70 yards in a N.W. direction, and its extremity is unlit.) The holding is good (sandy bottom) and shelter is sufficient to protect a yacht against the prevailing *gregale* (N.E.) which often stirs up a small sea, whose reflection from the opposite shore makes boatwork sometimes difficult.

Facilities. There are two restaurants close by. In the small village, ten minutes' walk, fresh provisions may be bought, and ice obtained from the factory near Giardini station for which transport is necessary. Buses ply irregularly to Taormina—about forty minutes' journey.

Known as Naxos, this small port, named after the early Greek colonists from the Aegean island of Naxos, is used only by a few small fishing craft. Tourists from Taormina come down here to bathe. Although less attractive, Naxos is safer for a yacht to berth than Mazzaro Bay; the water is clean and one can bathe from the yacht.

EAST COAST

Riposto is a deserted little wine port with an uninteresting village. Under normal conditions it is well-sheltered and only with northerly winds or strong easterlies is it most uncomfortable.

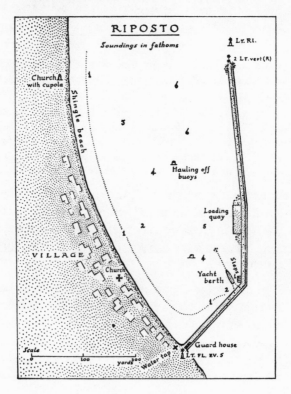

The coastline at Trapani

A fishing boat approaching the port of Trapani

The castle at Erice, Trapani

Approach. Chart 188—plan. There is no difficulty day or night. There is deep water inside the breakwater until near the elbow in the S.E. corner.

Berth stern to the quay as convenient, but bear in mind that towards the southern arm the harbour is slowly silting.

Facilities. Although provisions may be bought, the village is without interest. One may take the train or bus to Taormina—half an hour. The surrounding valley is rich in vegetation.

Coming south into Catania Bay easterly winds or calms may be expected, but there is nearly always a disturbed and bumpy sea caused by gusts from the high land around Mount Etna.

Catania, Sicily's second largest port, is unattractive and rather dirty. It is, however, the safest port on the east coast of Sicily, although according to Sailing Directions, it is dangerous to enter in a S.E. gale.

Approach and Berth. Chart 187 and plan on 181. Proceed to Porto Nuovo where there is space for yachts and small craft. The quay situated on Molo di Levante has depths of about 4 fathoms except at the S.W. end which shoals.

Facilities. Water, obtainable by hydrant on the quay, is said to be fresh spring water from the mountains. Fuel is available at W. end of fishing port, but if quantities of less than 500 gallons are bought Customs and Port charges outweigh the advantage of 'duty-free'. At the end of the quay is a small hut called the Club House, where a cold shower may be obtained.

A very good market is situated about 200 yards from the harbour entrance nearest the Port Office. The town, largely modern, has many good shops.

Although the oldest Sicilian city, Catania with a population of 387,000 has suffered much from various afflictions—earthquakes, inundations of lava, and eruptions from Etna, so that little remains of what Romans, Saracens and Normans erected. Every time the city has been obliterated, it has been rebuilt exactly on the same vulnerable site, the last reconstruction in 1669 embodies the modern conception of wide streets and public squares. Perhaps the most remarkable object in this town is the lava elephant flanked by an obelisk of Egyptian granite, originating from the late Roman period; this stands in the main square by the cathedral and town hall. The elephant was the symbol of the Catanians, but the theme of this statue was copied by Napoleon and used for decoration on a number of Parisian buildings.

Catania's present prosperity has been augmented by the discovery of oil and natural gas.

The Catanian Plain, north and west of the town has invariably been a malarial area; General Eisenhower in the Second World War complained bitterly of his army's casualties from this scourge.

One of the few reasons for visiting Catania is to make the ascent of Mt. Etna. Its summit is now 9,180 feet, but nearly a century ago it stood 1,500 feet higher.

In winter, its northern slopes have recently been exploited for ski-ing, arrangements being made with the Italian Alpine Club; but in summer, after May, one may ascend the mountain on foot, or by the 8.0 a.m. bus which takes one to the Rifugio Sapienza (one and three-quarter hours) and thence by cable car to the Observatory. Here one may spend the night in the C.A.I. refuge (*Casa degli Inglesi*), built originally in 1811 by the British army of occupation; beds and a small restaurant provide sufficient comfort. From the Observatory to the summit is an hour's walk, but one should start about two hours before dawn in order to see firstly the red hot lava flowing from the crater and then, proceeding to the summit, the wonderful view as sunrise draws near—Calabria, the Aeolian Islands, and the whole of Sicily are revealed in the rays of the rising sun. There are many other interesting climbs to be made on Mt. Etna, details of which are obtainable from the local C.A.I.

During the last century the local people in the village at the foot of Etna made a lucrative business of selling snow both to Malta and Italy. It fetched between a penny and threepence per pound.

Bruccoli. A small calanque inlet suitable for a yacht of small draught—scarcely worth a special visit.

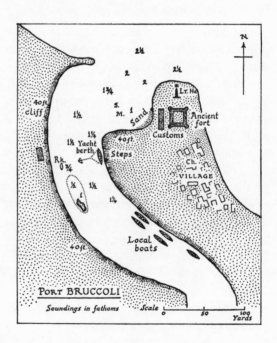

PORT BRUCCOLI

Soundings in fathoms · *Scale*

Approach. Run in on the lighthouse, and then keeping in mid-channel enter inside the inlet. (A yacht exceeding 6-feet draught is advised not to enter.)

Berth. There is only sufficient space to berth alongside the cliff by the steps as shown in the plan. The holding is mostly soft mud. Although a swell may enter the outer part of the inlet, its effect inside is negligible; but a large swell outside might prevent one from getting out through the entrance. A number of small fishing-boats berth inside the creek.

Facilities. At a poor hamlet close by bread and vegetables can be bought.

The little port was once busy with the export of wheat, tunny and building stone, but today it is idle, and the medieval castle, with its rounded towers at each corner, is the only reminder of its former importance. The local urchins who frequent the cliffside are apt to be a nuisance to a visiting yacht.

Porto di Augusta. A large area enclosed by low rough moles with many mooring buoys, refineries, cement works and tankers. The large commercial section of the port used by many tankers is Port Megarese, but no yacht would normally want to call here when the more attractive Syracuse lies only 12 miles southwards, and for small yachts the Porto Bruccoli even nearer.

Approach. See Chart 181. Leading lights, described in Sailing Directions, give a line of approach (274° true) through the main entrance; this must be closely followed as the lighted towers are set back inside the harbour about 150 yards beyond the low ends of the moles themselves. In March, 1808, the British sloop *Electra*, sixteen guns, struck this reef; the ship was lost, but all the crew saved.

Anchor according to the wind direction, in the north corner of the port in 3 fathoms on mud. This berth is well clear of shipping.

Facilities. The port is some distance from the shops, but the town offers all facilities.

There is an extensive naval area, formerly an important seaplane base for Imperial Airways on their route to India and East Africa. The port, which used to be a naval base, still shows some of the old defences; its traditional commercial use has been the export of salt.

Syracuse, an attractive, historic and ancient city with convenient berthing arrangements for a yacht in normal summer weather.

Approach. Charts 182 and 187. There is no difficulty day or night. A yacht should proceed towards the quay N. of Harbour Office.

Berth. Lay out anchor to the west and haul in stern to the quay. Well sheltered from easterly winds, but somewhat exposed to those from other directions especially W. winds from across the bay. Though lifted by the tall houses behind the quay, a strong wind with a fetch of 1½ miles stirs up an uncomfortable lop.

Note: The small fishing port entered 1 mile north of the main port is completely sheltered, but affords depths of only 8 feet.

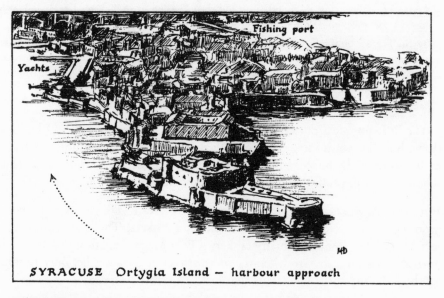

SYRACUSE Ortygia Island — harbour approach

Officials. Health, Harbour and Customs are all conveniently close.

Facilities. Water may be obtained by hydrant in a corner S. of the steamer quay. Fuel can be bought from a pump near the basin—there are plenty of shops within ten minutes' walk. Some good restaurants and trattorias are to be found near the main square (with the fountain). Hotels, where baths can be had, are close behind the quay above the Fountain of Arethusa. Alas, the famous fountain is a disappointment: the springs have long since dried up and the place has become an unattractive ditch of green water with a few papyrus leaves, carp and ducks. The well-known Hotel Villa Politi, 2 miles from the port, is still of high standard, but very expensive. Package tours now come to the other hotels within the town.

The modern city of 80,000 people is of moderate attraction. There is still plenty to see of the early city: the catacombs dating from early Christian times when St. Paul spent three days here; the 'Ear of Dionysius' by the quarries where the Athenian prisoners were confined; the Roman amphitheatre built a hundred years later. Of the Greek remains, although much has been quarried by successive generations, there are still columns of the temples and the theatre (where plays are occasionally performed), and Euryalus's castle, one of the 4th-century B.C. defences. From the castle one has a splendid panorama of the remains of the ancient city. On the island of Ortygia are the remains of columns from the temple of Apollo, and in the town above the harbour one can see how the Doric columns of the Temple of Athena have been incorporated into the cathedral in a most remarkable manner. Fortunately Cicero's description of its original form still survives; with 'doors of ivory and gold', it was enriched with beautiful sculpture and paintings, particularly the exploits of Agathocles (Sicilian hero) in twenty-seven pictures and portraits, and the figure of the great goddess above give one an idea of how it appeared as a place of worship many centuries ago. The famous meridian of Archimedes is said to have stood in the same building.

History. Since the 8th century B.C. when the early Greek settlers came here from Corinth, this city has had more interesting events in its history than most places. Because there is still so much material evidence of them to be seen today, it is worth describing them more fully.

The earliest stone construction is the remains of the long surrounding walls—about 14 miles—of Dionysius I, built to defend a city of perhaps half a million people (at least five or six times as large as it is today). It was then the largest fortified city of the Greek world, whose commerce alone demanded the protection of three hundred warships, and when it seemed that she was to be involved in war with Athens, engineers from Greece, Italy and Carthage were summoned to advise on the defences; thus, when the Athenian expedition started its attack in 415 B.C., the Syracusans were well prepared. The long siege, so fully described by Thucydides, might well have ended indecisively had not the Syracusan navy adopted the successful plan, of blocking the mouth of the harbour with a line of triremes broadside on together with merchant ships and other craft at anchor—thus locking in the besiegers. The Athenians soon realised that they must force their way out through this barrage, and no sooner had they started on this attempt than the Syracusans, although outnumbered, fell upon them with every ship they could muster. For a long while the issue was in the balance, but finally Athenian resistance was overcome and their whole fleet captured or sunk—the remnants of the army, unable to escape overland, were rounded up, the generals executed and 40,000 prisoners taken to become slaves or die in the quarries.

Some two hundred years later, Syracuse was less fortunate for, having quarrelled with Rome, an army under Marcellus was sent to conquer the city. At this time the famous philosopher and scientist Archimedes was a citizen of Syracuse and, apart from his scientific discoveries (the law of displacement, etc.), he devised a number of war machines, the most important being large stone-throwing catapults; it is also said that he invented a huge mirror to deflect the sun's rays on to the sails of besieging warships and thus set them on fire. The siege lasted two years, at the end of which Syracuse yielded; Archimedes was killed by Roman soldiers 'while working on a mathematical problem'. After Marcellus's conquest no Syracusan was allowed to live in Ortygia.

This was the end of Hellenic Sicily. The Romans exploited her commercially, but gradually the great city shrivelled up to become what it is today: the island town of Ortygia and the desolate plain of the one-time Outer City. In addition to the remains of the Greek period already described—walls, quarries, cave, theatre, temples—underwater enthusiasts have brought up what they claim to be evidence of the 'torches', i.e. Greek Fire. Of the Roman epoch, there are parts of dwellings and an amphitheatre; both St. Peter and St. Paul came here.

After many centuries without event, Syracuse received the defeated Dutch fleet after 1676 and provided the grave for Admiral de Reuter, who had been killed in action by the French. In 1798 Nelson spent five days here watering and provisioning his fleet before setting off to find the French, then in Egyptian waters supporting Napoleon's army.

Marzameni, is a pleasant bay, well sheltered from westerly winds, but without anything of interest ashore.

> **Approach.** Chart 187. The bay is divided by an island; the northern part is the more convenient for landing at the village. By day the approach is simple, but by night care is needed as the light is exhibited on the *centre* of the breakwater. The southern part of the bay has now been formed into a port with two moles, leaving an entrance in the N.E. which, when approaching from N., is difficult to distinguish. (See *M. &. P*)
>
> **Anchorage recommended.** Let go in the centre of the northern bay in 2 fathoms. There is convenient landing at the village; alternatively, enter the new harbour (with 10-foot depths at the entrance) and anchor inside.
>
> **Facilities.** The small village has a few general shops with limited supplies. Water is available at a tap at the northern landing place, but there is no restaurant.

From the new port the village is a twenty-minute walk, but it has nothing of interest. The bay is suitable for bathing and near the end of the southern mole one is clear of the usual local sightseers who normally throng the quay close to a visiting yacht.

Beyond Cape Passero the coast trends towards the west, becoming generally low and arid, and seen from a yacht one might imagine oneself off the coast of Africa. Close beyond the cape one must beware of extensive tunny nets which during early summer are laid out in a S.E. direction. The winds to be expected are westerly in the spring, tending later to become south and S.W.

SOUTH COAST

Porto Palo. A useful anchorage on the S.E. corner of Sicily. Of no particular interest, the port is much used by trawlers and can be useful to a yacht awaiting a fair wind to Malta.

Approach. See Chart 187. By day this is easy, and by night Spadero Light makes a convenient line of approach. A light is exhibited at the extremity of the mole which is 130 yards in length extending from the western point of the bay in a westerly direction. There is 3 fathoms depth just clear of the end, and 2 fathoms more than half way along its shoreward side clear of the ballasting. Although ringbolts are provided, these berths are unsuitable for a yacht to secure to.

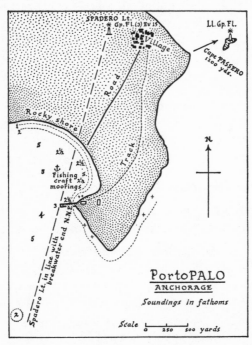

Anchorage. There is 2½ fathoms depth on a firm sandy bottom to within 100 yards of the shore along the eastern side of the bay. Within 50 yards of the shore the depth decreases to a fathom and the sand gives way to boulders and weed; the shore itself is inconveniently rocky for landing from the dinghy. Although open between south and west, the shelter from N. and E. is excellent.

Facilities. There is only a Customs guard-house and a small wine factory at the landing. Twenty minutes' walk brings one to the small hamlet of Spadero with its lighthouse and Meteorological Station. The shops here are very primitive, but a bus runs to the next village, Pichino, and here is connection with Syracuse.

Since the Punic Wars no mention can be found of this useful anchorage except as a refuge for local craft during strong N. winds. During the last two centuries it was often used by Maltese vessels awaiting a fair wind to cross the channel to Valletta.

Gela, once important as a town by the sea, has now become a commercial seaport and a summer resort for the Sicilians. A long jetty has recently been built to accommodate oil-tankers, and the dry cargo jetty is being extended, but the place is quite unsuitable for a yacht. Already an inner port with depths of 2 fathoms accommodates smaller vessels which load with grain and bitumen. The recent industrial activity, largely due to the discovery of oil after the Second World War, has brought about a great expansion of the port whose population has now grown to 60,000. On the nearby beaches American troops landed in July 1943 to drive the Germans out of Sicily. (See *M. & P.*)

Licata is a trawler port, often very dirty, and affording nothing attractive. Its shelter should be sought only in event of necessity.

Approach. Chart 187 and plan on 2113. The approach is easy by day or night.

Berth. Having entered the port, steer for 'Beacon' marked on chart, and berth stern to the eastern wall near the main lighthouse. There are depths of about 20 feet at the jetties.

Facilities. Though there is a hydrant on the quay, there is not always water. There are good shops for provisions nearby and an ice factory. The albergo has a restaurant which provides a good dinner at reasonable cost.

Porto Empedocle, a medium size commercial port—safe, but dirty and unattractive. It is useful for shelter when visiting the temples of Agrigento.

Approach. Chart 2113 with plan. Proceed into the inner harbour.

Berth. There is a choice of berthing either by the signal station, or where the harbour-launches moor up. The bottom is soft mud and the water very dirty.

Officials. The Capitaneria lies along the shore to the westward of the root of the mole.

Facilities. Provisions can be bought in the small town adjoining the port. There are a couple of restaurants and bars, 15 minutes' walk on top of the long breakwater. Ice is obtainable at a factory here too. It is most unwise to leave a yacht unattended and a *vigilante* (watchman) should be hired, through the medium of the Harbour Master, when leaving the boat empty. Steamers run daily to the islands of Linosa, Lampedusa and Pantelleria.

The port is busy with shipments of sulphur and salt, and is frequented by mischievous urchins, whose presence near a visiting yacht calls for the greatest vigilance. Many fishing craft also use the place. The small uninspiring town which spreads itself around the port is named after the great philosopher, scientist, poet and perhaps magician, Empedocles, who was at the height of his career about 440 B.C. One of his most useful achievements was the establishment of the School of Medicine, and one of his important scientific discoveries was that air is a separate substance; but he also became famous in legend for having thrown himself into the crater of Etna.

With a population of nearly 50,000 people **Agrigento** stands on the ridge above Porto Empedocle and until 1927 was known by the Saracen name of

Girgenti. It is only a shadow of the former Greek city, whose ruins lie on a site so vast (2 square miles are enclosed within the walls) that it is difficult to know, without the guide-book, where to begin the tour; one should, however, devote at least a whole day to visiting the temples. Buses from the port run every half hour, and take twenty minutes to reach the upper part of the hill, giving access to the temples. Ascending from the sea Virgil wrote of the 'majestic line of escarpments crowned with mighty walls'.

In early times, when known as Camicos, the Cretans besieged Agrigento unsuccessfully for five years. The city expanded enormously during Greek colonial days. 'They built as though they meant to live for ever' wrote Empedocles; and at the time of the Roman Empire, Agrigento had become a city of nearly a quarter of a million people. But the decline soon set in, and before being overrun by the Saracens, many temples had already started to crumble on account of earthquake tremors. When Roger the Norman came in the 11th century, the place was again set in order and a bishopric established.

Sciacca. An old and primitive town, standing on a steep hill overlooking a shallow and crowded fishing port.

> **Approach.** Chart 186. The safest approach is from the S.E. end of the detached mole to the W. end of the harbour breakwater. Here the depths are barely 2 fathoms, which continue up the middle of the harbour. The harbour breakwater has been recently rebuilt, and a more powerful white light—Fl. (2)—established on the N.W. extension, visible 6 to 8 miles.
>
> **Berth.** The port is very shallow, especially towards the sides, by the quays, which are usually crammed with trawlers. One may anchor off the detached mole, but here the bottom is rocky, except for a patch of sand 50 yards E. of its northern extremity. This position is suitable only in calm and settled weather. (See *M. & P.*)
>
> **Facilities.** Provisions are best obtained from the town up on the hill.

There may be two hundred small trawlers in this little port. All are painted turquoise blue and the fishermen are usually to be seen busily mending nets, slipping and repairing their boats. The quays are crowded with ill-mannered urchins, and close behind are the squalid dwellings of the port. The Aragonese town standing on the slopes of Monte San Calogero above, is a pleasure after the port, and now has a population of more than 30,000. The large, shaded square affords a fine view over the harbour with its many fishing craft below. The cathedral, of Norman influence, has little of the original work remaining, and the Spanish castle is a mere shell.

Called by the Romans Thermae Salinunte, the hot springs are still active on the hill east of the town, and have maintained the town's reputation as a thermal resort. Legend relates that King Minos of Crete was stifled in them. Nowadays, the thermal baths attract only those suffering from rheumatism; far more visitors bathe at the white sandy beach east of the town.

The great Greek city of **Selinunte,** whose ruins lie on the coast is only 10 miles W.N.W. of Sciacca. From seaward, the columns may be seen standing out boldly close above the shore but there is no suitable place for landing. Approaching by road you first pass some disused vineyards and then enter a fertile, flowering valley, with lemons, almonds and olives. The main colonnade of Doric columns stands close to the shore, and is seen against a background of deep-blue sea. As well as the colonnade, there are huge blocks of masonry, broken drums of columns—all a reminder of the sack of this beautiful Greek city by the Carthaginians in the 5th century B.C. Many of the best pieces of sculpture, especially the metopes, which have survived the intervening centuries have been recovered and taken to the National Museum at Palermo.

Continuing westwards one soon comes to the low-lying **Cape Granitola** with its tall lighthouse, which during early summer months should be passed at a distance of about 2 miles to the S.W. on account of the extensive tunny nets. This Cape, which until about a hundred years ago was unlit, was a great danger to shipping. Early in the last century many foreign ships were wrecked; the British navy lost three brigs, *Rocket, Hermes* and *John,* the sloop *Ceres* and three merchantmen. The lighthouse was not erected until 1853.

A number of shoals caused by volcanic action lie some miles to the south-ward of this cape—one is of particular interest: lying 25 miles south of Cape Granitola is the *Terrible Bank* with the *Graham Shoal* now covered by 4 fathoms of water. This shoal is in fact the submerged top of a volcano and in August 1831 it burst its way upward to become an island 180 feet high; but within three months it had again subsided to become a shoal.

Mazara del Vallo. A harbour formed by the mouth of the River Mazara, was made into a port to accommodate a large fleet of trawlers. Although the inner part affords perfect shelter, the place is very crowded.

Approach. Chart 186 and Italian Chart 262, plan. (The outer mole is now joined to the eastern mole by a bridge not shown on the chart.) On entering the inner pier-heads, keep to the starboard or eastern side, leaving to port a small black tower and a red conical buoy, both marking shoal water. (See *M. & P.*)

Berth. Proceeding up harbour and rounding the bend to port, it may be necessary to secure alongside a trawler. A berth on the west side is quieter, but further from the town, than one on the east side. At the quays there are depths of 9 feet.

Facilities. Some good shops and a supermarket some distance east of the river. A bridge crosses a short distance above the berths.

The port of Mazara del Vallo has for many years been remarkable for the *Marrobio*—a form of small tidal wave which quickly raises the level of the sea about 2 feet when rising water rushes into the creeks and inlets. In a few minutes the water recedes and then the cycle repeats itself about every ten minutes and may perhaps continue for a couple of hours. It is a form of *seiche* and is usually accompanied by humid conditions, a falling barometer and a change to southerly weather. This phenomenon has been experienced at other Mediterranean ports, viz. Ciudadela in Minorca, Bonifacio in Corsica and Galaxidhi in the Gulf of Corinth. It can be very dangerous for a yacht moored in the normal manner, stern to a quay, and one should take precautions if these weather conditions obtain.

Mazara del Vallo, founded by the early Greeks of nearby Selinunte, has now become a flourishing fishing port with nearly 40,000 inhabitants. The present town is old, with a domed baroque cathedral, campanile, and the bishop's palace. Close by is a pleasant square, and here at the foot of the seminary stands the statue of St. Vitus, the patron saint of Mazara commemorated by a colourful festival, held annually on 15th June. As the son of a Sicilian nobleman he suffered martyrdom at an early age in the latter part of the 3rd century by which time he had acquired a limited reputation for being able to cure certain diseases including those contracted from animals. His name did not become generally known until the 9th century when, especially in Germany, a cult was established and the name of the saint was invoked against the neurotic disorder of chorea, soon to become known as St. Vitus's Dance. Every year his silver image is taken from the church and embarked in a fishing boat which, after cruising round the harbour, proceeds to the Salami River where most of the population are gathered for the landing. To the accompaniment of the beating of drums, firing of guns, playing of loud music by the town band, as well as the acclaim of the people, the silver image is then returned in procession to the church.

For a long time Mazara del Vallo was the embarkation port used by the knights when crossing to Malta.

WEST COAST

Marsala. A well-sheltered commercial port for the export of wine, with a town of no particular interest.

Approach. Chart 2113. Entry is straightforward. A yacht should proceed to the furthest basin. In unsettled weather strong, variable currents are reported.

Berth at a new quay north of the Harbour Office in 2½ fathoms. Lay out anchor towards the breakwater on a mud bottom. With the exception of a swell in Sirocco winds, shelter is good.

Facilities. Fresh water is laid on by hydrant at the quay. A provision store is close by and shops in the town, fifteen minutes' walk. Hotel with restaurant is ten minutes' walk from the quay.

Marsala, originally a Phoenician town and subsequently a great Sicilian base for Carthage and Rome, was called Marsa Ali (Port Ali) in Arab days. Livy describes how the Romans once blocked it with stones, and again the Venetians blocked it at the time of Lepanto to deny its use to the Turks. With the development of Trapani in recent centuries, Marsala at first declined; but when the wine trade was established in 1773 by George Woodhouse and Ingham Whitaker it began to recover and the present town-hall square was built at this time. The stones blocking the inner port were removed but, until the harbour was enlarged much later, ships had to anchor outside. In the Napoleonic Wars when the British fleet could no longer call at Spanish ports to buy sherry they turned to the white wine of Marsala instead. Italian firms now operate this trade, and small tankers may be seen filling up with shipments of wine. But the fortified 'after dinner' form of sherry, which for more than a century used to satisfy many an impoverished young naval officer, appears to have only a limited export to England nowadays.

The town which took a hard knock from bombs in the Second World War has recovered and supports a population of 80,000. The cathedral (dedicated to St. Thomas à Becket), and some Baroque churches survived, and are of limited interest; but the old English church, badly damaged by bombs, has now been abandoned.

The greatest historical event in Marsala took place on 11th May, 1860, when Garibaldi's two small ships, *Piedmonte* and *Lombardo*, crammed with north Italian patriots, steamed into port before the very eyes of two Neapolitan warships. *Lombardo* was unfortunate in grounding at the entrance, but she managed to land her men and ammunition before her opponents were able to fire on her. Four days later 'The Thousand' were opposing a strong force of government troops on Piantoclei Romani where Garibaldi, by extreme skill and subterfuge, compelled 20,000 well-conditioned troops to surrender. This remarkable feat brought Garibaldi to the zenith of his military career; he won the sympathy of all Sicilians, and throughout Sicily today there is still hardly a town or village without a statue or bust of Garibaldi, or at least a street named after this national hero.

ISLANDS OFF SOUTHERN SICILY

(Seldom visited by a yacht except en route to Malta)

These consist of Pantelleria and the three small and unimportant Pelagie Islands—Linosa, Lampione and Lampedusa.

It is seldom a yacht visits these places, except perhaps Pantelleria the most important and the most convenient at which to call when proceeding to Malta.

Island of Pantelleria. A volcanic island with a small harbour for fishing craft. It is sometimes useful to a yacht as a port of call between Tunis and Malta.

> **Approach.** Chart 193, plan. Make for the Western Harbour, being careful on entering to keep close to the end of the mole on account of the water shoaling towards the shore. One can only come here in reasonably settled weather.
>
> **Berth.** Secure at the inner corner of the basin with anchor to seaward and stern to the rough stonework of the mole. Here is good shelter and adequate depths close to the mole; but the bottom is either stone or rock, on sand, and one should buoy the anchor.
>
> **Facilities.** Provisions and other supplies can be bought at shops on the waterfront where there are also some small restaurants. There is steamer communication with Empedocle, Trapani and Tunis. Air connection with Sicily.

The buildings in the small port have been rebuilt since the Second World War and a number of skyscrapers now stand, somewhat grotesquely, close to the waterfront. The mountain slopes are surprisingly green and many are cultivated with vineyards and market-garden produce; peasant cottages are sprinkled on the mountain sides. Inland a number of extinct volcano heads may be seen.

Returning again to the Sicilian coast and sailing northwards towards Trapani one must stand well away from the coast because of the shallows off Stagnoni—a large area of salt-pans, windmills and pyramids of salt.

Trapani. A clean fishing harbour with a growing town and shore excursions.

> **Approach.** See Chart 189 and 2113 with harbour plan. [Photographs facing p. 112.]
>
> **Berth.** Berth off the Customs House with anchor to the southward in 4 fathoms and stern to the quay. The bottom is mud and the holding uncertain. The harbour, formerly exposed to S.W., has recently been improved by extending the southern breakwater. The day breeze starts in the South following the sun round to West.
>
> **Officials.** Harbour Master and Customs.
>
> **Facilities.** There is an excellent daily market, and provisions shops are conveniently near the quay. Water may be obtained through the medium of the Harbour Master; in 1967 it was supplied by the Fire Services free of charge. Ice can be got at a small depot ten minutes' walk from the quay.

The town, largely modernized on the gridiron pattern, has a population of 80,000, many of whom are occupied with exports of salt, tunny, oil and wine. A shipyard and a canning factory adjoin the port which gives little indication of the large-scale industry recently developed to the northward.

There are many fishing craft and a fleet of small local sailing coasters based on the port. These boats with a large lateen and two headsails are usually handled by one man; they load salt from the nearby salt pans and bring it to the quays for shipment. A few *tartanes* remain in service ferrying salt, carefully sealed by the Customs, to the canning factory at Favignana. In Roman days coral divers were based here, for Trapani exported 'the most highly appreciated coral', a trade which continues today, together with a small export of alabaster. Wine under the trade name of *Marsala* is also exported.

At the harbour entrance the remains of its strong medieval defences can still be seen—the fortified tower on Ligny Point, and on the islet of Colombaia the stump of the original castle-lighthouse built many centuries ago. This rocky islet is referred to by Virgil in his history of Aeneas whom, he claims, landed here on his voyage from Carthage to celebrate the funeral rites of his father Anchises.

The old Aragonese village of Erice lies on the summit of Mount St. Giuliano (2,500 feet). [See photograph facing page 113.] From here is a magnificent view of the Aegadean Islands. The medieval village with its three churches, the flagged streets and a grey Norman castle, partly quarried from the Temple of Venus, is on top but largely hidden by pines. One may drive there by car in forty minutes, or take the cable car; it makes a pleasant excursion, especially on a hot evening, when one may dine in the cool air at one of the restaurants above. Since ancient times Eryx has been regarded as an impregnable fortress with a fine look-out over the seas. It was widely associated with the worship of Aphrodite, and legends have been handed down of the many sailors who found their way to this holy shrine. This Temple of Venus, however, was torn down in the 14th century and the Chiesa Matrice with campanile, porch and rose window now stands in its place.

In the 11th century, when Roger the Norman besieged Eryx, he is said to have dreamed of St. Julian, hence its name for centuries—San Giuliano, which reverted in Mussolini's day to Erice.

AEGADEAN ISLANDS (*Isole Egadi*)

The three Aegadean Islands lying within 20 miles of Sicily's west coast are tall, largely steep-to and, excepting Favignana, are sparsely inhabited. The few partially sheltered anchorages are used by local fishing craft. The inhabitants are mostly occupied in fishery, especially tunny fishing and canning.

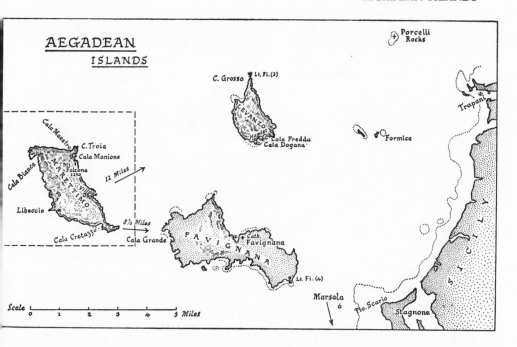

In the channels the currents flow either towards N.E. (mostly in summer) or S.W., according to the wind. Tunny nets may partially obstruct the channels in the spring months.

During summer there is often thick haze lying over the islands, making them difficult to discern when making a landfall.

The Agadean Islands have, for a long time, been the centre of the Sicilian tunny fishing. For two centuries they were owned by the Pallavincini family of Genoa, but a hundred years ago Signor Florio of Palermo bought them and his organization operated the fishing industry until recent years. Florio's statue still stands in the main square of Favignana village, and his pretentious villa, now neglected, is at the quayside.

Communication with all three islands is maintained by the daily ferry-steamer from Trapani, and there are frequent daily hydrofoil services with Favignana and Levanzo. In the autumn months Sicilian sportsmen with guns and dogs may be seen crossing from Trapani, for many migrating birds rest on the islands during their passage southwards.

Island of Favignana has a primitive fishing village, with a sheltered anchorage off the main port:

127

Approach. Charts 189 and 2113 with plan. The signal tower on the hill is conspicuous, and Sailing Directions give clear instructions. During the tunny season in the spring it is often difficult to avoid the off-lying nets. Sometimes during summer there is haze off this coast, and the consequent very poor visibility may cause anxiety. When making a landfall, Cape Bon and Palermo Airport radio beacons can be helpful.

Anchorage or Berth. A yacht may anchor off the pier on a sandy patch in 3 fathom depths, but the holding is fine sand and not always good. Since the extension of the stone pier it is now possible to berth inside or outside the head of the jetty in $2\frac{1}{2}$ fathoms. The hydrofoil quay and the steamer quay must be avoided. Shelter, during the summer months, is invariably good.

Officials. Harbour Master and Customs.

Facilities. The village shops sell some stores and provisions. Limited water can be had at the quay, but no ice. There is no proper restaurant, only some bars and a few cafés. A small summer hotel attracts a few visitors. Frequent ferry and hydrofoil services from Trapani daily.

The village which houses most of the island's 5,000 inhabitants is unpretentious, but has a well kept main square and orderly little shops. Tunny fishing is the main occupation and there is a constant demand for labour at the canning factory. In the autumn months when tunny fishing in the Mediterranean is no longer practicable the fish are carried here in special freighters from northern Norway, from Spain and even Japan; they are then cut up and canned in the factory, the cheap labour and local oil making it a profitable venture.

In earlier times when the harbour sheltered the galleys of successive overlord states, it was protected by three forts, sited on the surrounding hills. Only the Aragonese fort, Sta. Caterina, now remains. Standing prominently on the hill it now houses a signal station; the ascent (1,000 feet) on a clear day is rewarding for the fine view across the island towards the Sicilian coast. In the port one notices the well constructed galley sheds; these are said to have been adapted in Florio's time to house the tunny lighters.

Known as Aegusa (Goat Island) in classical times, Favignana Island has been associated by students of the *Aeneid* with Ulysses's landfall after his voyage from the 'Land of the Lotus-eaters'—Djerba. Ulysses thought it a luxuriant island and described it as 'covered with woods and the home of innumerable goats'. Favignana still grazes goats, but is hardly luxuriant today and, despite some fresh water springs, is very dried-up in summer and tankers must bring water supplies from Trapani. Until a hundred years ago the whole western plain of the island, still named Il Busco on the chart, was a forest of pines, but today it is almost bare with very little cultivation. Part of it is a resting place for migratory birds in spring and autumn. The island, during the summer months, presents a barren appearance.

Of other anchorages on the Favignana coast, the only one of interest to a yacht is

Cala Grande. It lies close S. of Pta. Sottile lighthouse and has a moderately sheltered anchorage close by a summer hotel. This place is not for large yachts.

> **Approach.** Some white houses are the only discernible objects, and one should approach on a course of about 075° to pass a cable northward to them. Closing into the bay a low rocky spur may be seen projecting N.W. of the houses. The extremity of this should be left to starboard before turning into the small cove.
>
> **Anchorage.** Anchor should be let go about 100 yards from the houses (and hotel) in about 3 fathoms. The bottom is thick weed on sand. Open only between W.S.W. through W. to N.W., but even a strong Sirocco sends in a swell.
>
> **Facilities.** Ulysses Hotel provides good meals, and comfortable accommodation for about seventy summer guests. Underwater fishing is one of the attractions. Communication by road with Favignana.

Island of Levanzo, lying 3 miles north of Favignana, is tall, rugged and barren with two small coves in the south, where one can anchor with good holding in convenient depths.

Dogana Cove is charming; the small houses of the hamlet stand by the waterfront at the foot of a steep hill rising to 900 feet. Here a medium-sized yacht can anchor in 3 fathom depths with thick weed on sand. Land in the dinghy at a short mole where the fishing-boats berth.

About two hundred people live in the hamlet which now has a modest summer inn, but little else. Both the Trapani ferry and the hydrofoil boat call daily.

At the N. end of the island, and reached by a track passing through the *macchi*, is a cave by the sea concealed in a precipice which is not easy to find. In the cave are prehistoric drawings of horses and fish.

Fredda Cove is a similar anchorage, but less attractive than Dogana Cove. Neither are possible anchorages in Sirocco winds.

Towards Trapani are the Formiche Islets:

Islet of Formiche is the eastern one of two low lying islets recognized by the old tower and buildings used for hauling up tunny boats and for fishery stores. On the south side of the islet is a very small boat harbour, but close outside it the ground is foul with large rocks. If interested in a closer look at these old buildings, a yacht may find temporary anchorage S.E. of the tower in 5 fathoms on a sandy bottom, and one can then land in the dinghy at the boat harbour. This expedition is hardly worth the bother, but it is difficult to avoid being inquisitive at the unusual sight of solid old buildings appearing to grow out of the sea on this minute islet.

Tunny nets are laid out from here to the S.E. during the spring.

Island of Marettimo, the westernmost of the Aegadean Islands, is tall, barren and steep-to, with only a small village and some indifferent anchorages. One anchorage of interest to a yacht lies on the N.E. corner of the island:

Cala Manione

Approach. The small castle on Troia Point (used as an emergency signal station) is an easy mark by day: but by night it is impossible to find the way into the anchorage.

Anchorages. Chart 189. Fifty yards off the neck of the isthmus are depths of 10 fathoms shoaling to 5 as one approaches over a sandy bottom. A stern warp to the short mole is necessary. In a west to N.W. wind this anchorage is very snug, there being no swell. Should there be a sudden change to an easterly quarter one must put to sea. With southerly winds there are squalls from Mt. Falcone. One can shift to Cala Maestro on the N.W. side of Trois Pt., but being deep and rocky, this is not recommended.

The rocky coast under the castle is sometimes used by underwater fishermen. The castle was manned as a look-out by the British Navy during the Napoleonic Wars. When the French fleet was expected to be making for Egypt we read in the C.-in-C's journal: 'April 7th, 1805. H.M.S. *Seahorse* was sent to Marettimo to gain intelligence from the officer there.'

Other Anchorages of possible use to a yacht are:

(a) **Cala Bianca** sometimes used by fishermen.

(b) **Off the village** under C. San Simone; but the anchorage is poor and the only village, with about 1,000 inhabitants, an uninteresting little place. Two short piers extend seawards but provide no shelter for a vessel in the entirely exposed anchorage.

(c) **Cala Cretazzo,** lying at the foot of a cliff on the S.W. tip of the island, has convenient depths on a sandy bottom. It affords poor shelter and is inaccessible by land.

Today almost all the island's inhabitants live in the village; many are employed in the trawlers which catch and deliver fish at the west Sicilian ports.

The Skerki Bank with Keith Reef (depth under 6 feet), which lies some 52 miles to the west of Marettimo Island, was the cause of the total loss of H.M.S. *Athenian* (sixty-four guns) in October 1804. She was carrying despatches from London for Admiral Sir Sidney Smith—then at Palermo—who, hearing of the ship's loss, caused the shores of Marettimo to be searched trusting that valuable flotsam might be recovered. The search was successful and although three hundred and fifty one lives were lost the despatches eventually reached the Admiral. Many ships have been lost on this bank.

North Coast

Island of Ustica lying more than 30 miles north of the Sicilian shores is a volcanic, green island with a steep inaccessible coast. A bay on the south coast, close off the hamlet, is the only practical anchorage. In view of this limited shelter it seems hardly worthwhile for a yacht to make a special visit.

> **Approach.** Chart 170. In the distance, if approached from E. or W. it appears as two islands, and apart from the shoal on the N. coast it is safe to approach close-to.

> **Anchorage** is close offshore in Sta. Maria Cove on a sandy bottom in 3 fathoms. This is very exposed to southerly winds in which case it is advisable to put to sea rather than try anchoring elsewhere. The Trapani steamer calls here daily with passengers and provisions, and a hydrofoil service operates from Palermo all the summer months.

> **Facilities** are limited; a few modest hotels have recently grown up to accommodate foreign tourists, and some shops sell fresh provisions.

The island has a population of about 1,200 largely employed in cultivation. In Greek and Roman times it was called Osteodes (Island of Bones) because the Carthaginians once abandoned here a mercenary army of six thousand men.

The Northern Shores of Sicily begin at Cape San Vito with tall, bold, mountain ranges reaching up from the sea. For 120 miles this stretch of coast is extremely attractive and generally very green with cultivation in the valleys and foothills, the vineyards, lemon groves, olives and pinewoods are conspicuous. More than half a dozen ports are available for yachts as well as some less protected anchorages. The prevailing wind is N.W. becoming N.E. as one nears the eastern end of the coast. Off certain sections of the coast there is often a land breeze starting at dawn and continuing for about three hours.

San Vito is a recently built small fishing harbour inadequately protected by two moles. It lies close to a village with a modest summer hotel and sandy beach.

> **Approach and Anchorage.** Steer for the wide gap between the moles and let go the anchor when the extremity of the N.E. mole bears north-east. The depth here is 2½ fathoms and the bottom firm sand. There is room for a small yacht to swing, and at the same time have the advantage of shelter from the swell after the day breeze. A larger yacht must anchor outside where the holding is equally good. One can land in the dinghy at the quay.

> **Facilities.** A modest hotel stands on the waterfront and there are a few shops.

A fine sandy bathing beach runs round the bay. The village, which is of no interest, has 4,000 inhabitants mostly employed in the stone quarries, in fishing and in agriculture. The port serves little purpose except to accommodate a few small fishing craft, for the fishing in the vicinity is poor.

Castellammare del Golfo, a dull fishing port with a new harbour mole, is not worth a special visit.

Approach. Mount Inice, towering above the small town, is distinctive and there is no difficulty in finding the harbour, day or night. On approaching the extremity of the mole one should follow it along keeping at least 20 yards off because of broken masonry lying scattered over the bottom. The top of the breakwater was recently swept away by winter gales and no attempt had been made by 1967 to clear the obstruction.

Berth stern to a quay at the western end of the harbour, bows E.: but keep at least 20 yards from the N.W. corner which is shallow.

Facilities. A water-tap is permanently available 15 yards from the quayside. Provisions, wine, etc. can be bought in this somewhat straggly town which can be reached in twenty minutes from the harbour quay. A new motel on the west side of the town can provide meals, showers and accommodation. A good bus service operates to Palermo and Trapani.

The Sicilian town of Castellammare should not be mistaken for the more prosperous Castellammare di Stabia near Naples. Both ports are without interest for the visiting yacht; there are no colourful fishing craft or local craftsmanship, no restaurant or trattoria of particular appeal. One can perhaps understand this state in a northern commercial town, but it seems surprising in N.W. Sicily.

Castallammare del Golfo has a population of nearly 20,000 and is typical of other small towns in this poverty stricken area of N.W. Sicily where more than a third of the population is illiterate. Half the people are employed on agricultural work and take their children with them instead of sending them to school. A small percentage are fishermen, and the Rome government recently built them a substantial port, but this has now been largely destroyed by the winter gales. Earnings are on a low scale and, by the time the Mafia have their rake-off little remains to sustain a family, which lives at the lowest level, usually eating and sleeping in one room without even the convenience of a water supply, which must be fetched from a fountain in the street. One person in five is registered as destitute.

One can, however, leave the town and make a couple of interesting excursions into the country by car to:

(a) **Scopello** a small fishing village lying on the coast a short distance to the N.W. In the spring the inhabitants are busy with their *Tonnara*, the nets of which extend nearly a mile offshore. Visitors come in summer to see this remarkable rocky bay, and a number of underwater fishermen stay here at a small Motel.

(b) **Segesta.** The Doric temple and theatre is only half an hour's drive and well worth seeing. The temple, never quite finished, is reputed to have the finest proportions of any and lies in a perfect position in a broad valley with a rocky mountain behind it. The theatre, half an hour's walk uphill from the temple, is of the 1st century B.C. Segesta suffered the same fate as other Greek towns in Sicily: after seeking allies in Athens and later Carthage, she was conquered by Rome in the First Punic War.

Between Castellammare and Palermo are some unimportant anchorages suitable for a yacht only in settled weather:

Carini Bay which is rather open. Its anchorages are explained in Sailing Directions: the bay is beside the airport.

Femmine anchorage is off the village—not the islet, as its title implies. Although shelter is good, the holding—rock and weed—is poor.

Sferracavello—Chart 169, is a more suitable anchorage. The place is becoming a summer resort, but there is nothing particular to recommend.

Mondello Bay, beyond Cape Gallo, the smart summer resort for Palermo with its yacht and bathing clubs, hotels and restaurants, is a shallow bay, exposed to E. The bottom is rocky, and it is almost impossible for a yacht of, say, 6- or 8-feet draught to anchor near the centre of interest. The only suitable anchorage is N.N.E. of Celesi Point where the bottom is mostly sand; this is far out and very exposed. The local shallow draught motor-boats have a marina in the N.W. corner of the bay. If one wishes to visit Mondello Bay it seems to be more convenient to go by bus or car from Palermo.

Palermo, capital of Sicily, is a large city of considerable interest and a spacious commercial and passenger port.

Approach. Chart 169. No difficulty day or night.

Berth. Yachts now berth at south mole (Molo Meridionale) where Shell and Esso have their pumps; stern to the quay, and bows W., anchor on a mud bottom. Although the quay has now been tidied up the harbour here is usually filthy and often there is a large covering of oil. Shelter is good.

Officials. The large Port Authority building is by the steamer quays, at least twenty minutes' walk. A British Consul General has his office near the town centre. There is Club Canottieri but it does not help foreign yachts.

Facilities. At the south mole there is plenty of fresh water and fuel from Shell or Esso. Ice and laundry can be arranged by one of these agencies. Everything can be bought in the city, but shops are about twenty minutes' walk from the yacht berth. There is a useful market off Corso Vittorio Emmanuele. Many good restaurants in the city towards the opera; also self-service restaurant and bars. Summer cafés lie above the seafront beyond the root of the S. mole. Yachts used to complain of thieving at night, but in recent years police control has been improved.

La Cala, the basin beyond where the yachts berth, has become a graveyard for the last of the old wooden sailing craft. Some, still in trade, serve as sand barges, and one may see *trabaccoli* from the Adriatic, many *tartanes* and other small coasters which have seen better days. Pride in appearance has vanished, for the sailors know that when the building boom ends no further employment will be offered, and thus the gaudy paintwork and the canvas sails have already been sacrificed. Along the waterfront the old houses have been torn down to make way for the new motor road. This demolition has brought to light some fine old classical buildings, which the authorities have partially restored.

Palermo, an historic city with a population of 622,000, is also a great centre of communication by sea, land and air. Originally a Phoenician settlement and then capital of Carthaginian Sicily, it has continued as a flourishing city through-out the ages. A hundred years ago it came very near to being destroyed. This was in the summer of 1860 when Garibaldi's force, already in the higher out-skirts of the city, was about to attack the royalist defences within. Neapolitan warships had opened fire and damaged a number of buildings when H.M.S. *Hannibal* arrived with Admiral Mundy. He persuaded the two royalist generals and Garibaldi to meet on board. An armistice was subsequently signed after which there was no more bloodshed nor bombardment.

On landing at the port one finds that most of the old quarter as well as the city walls have been torn down and replaced by large blocks of flats; but much Norman–Byzantine architecture for which the city is famous still stands. Espec-ially fine are the Palazzo Reale, with its rare examples of Byzantine secular art, the cathedral, the Martorana and the Zisa Fountain. Most remarkable of all, however, are the perfectly preserved mosaics and painted ceiling of the cathedral of Monreale on the hill behind the city; the cloisters have especially beautiful twin marble columns. It is advisable to consult a guide-book as there is so much to be seen in this great city.

Proceeding eastwards from Palermo one soon comes to a promontory with mountains rising steeply from the sea to more than a thousand feet.

Rounding Cape Zefferano the coast trends southwards until reaching the well-sheltered little harbour of **Porticello.** An unspoilt little fishing port well worth a visit.

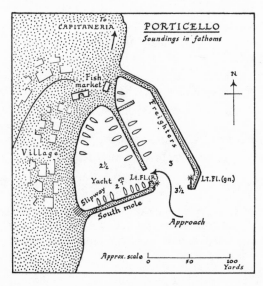

Approach and Berth. Chart 169 shows only a single breakwater, but there is also a southern mole which affords complete protection from east winds.

After rounding the outer molehead steer to the S.W. and enter the basin formed by the south mole which extends from the shore in a direction E.N.E. (towards the extremity of the outer molehead). There are depths of 2½ fathoms inside the basin and slightly less at the quay where one can secure the yacht's stern with bows pointing N.N.W. The bottom is mud and shelter all round. Both moleheads are lit. [Photograph facing p. 96.]

Officials. Harbour Master's office is north of the main quay.

Facilities. In the village there is not much to be bought, but barrow boys from the upper village sell fruit and vegetables most of the day. The fish market is open all day. Water is rationed in the village, and none is laid on at the quay; ice at the factory near the root of S. mole. Bus communications with Palermo every hour.

Porticello is a small and primitive fishing village, so far quite unspoilt. Adjoining it is the more modern part with a few scattered summer villas and a lido. One or two Palermo yachtsmen keep their motor-boats in the port which is very crowded already with many local fishing boats and a small type of trawler; nearly all are painted cobalt blue. Two small building yards construct an unusual type of boat with a curved sternpost projecting at least 3 feet above deck level and necessitating the boat being steered with an iron U-shaped tiller. Known locally as the *Dritto Poppa*, this sternpost resembles the high extended stern of the Maltese *dghaisa*. Local people believe it to be of Arab origin.

Following the main road up the mountainside towards Mt. Catalfano one comes to some ruins of Solunto, a former Phoenician town. They are of little interest but from here is a fine view along the coast.

The Sicilian shores now become less abrupt: the mountains recede from the coast leaving a green belt renowned for its lemon groves and vineyards. The white wine of Casteldaccia is quite the nicest in Sicily. Villages are spread along the coast and some modern villas have grown up. The castle of Trabia with its cranellated walls, 8 miles from Porticello, stands prominently by the sea, but the approach to its harbour is very shallow, and it shelters only a few boats.

Termini Imeresi a small commercial port with 3-fathom depths is largely silted. It is of no interest to a yacht save in emergency.

> **Approach and Berth.** Chart 170, plan. Keeping half a cable from the extremity of the breakwater, steer for a black conical buoy 2¼ cables S.S.E. (between the buoy and the breakwater are shallows where the sand has silted; you cannot enter by night as the buoy is unlit). From the buoy head for the extremity of south mole (Santa Lucia) and thence to the quay. There are depths of 3 fathoms in most of the approach channel and slightly less the W. side of the quay. The harbour continues to silt.

The town, built on the hill slope at the head of the harbour has a population of about 25,000, and is advertised as a summer bathing resort. It has many sky-scraper buildings and its appearance from seaward is ugly. Less than 2 miles eastward of the town is a new oil port with a long pier.

Cefalù. An old town with recent tourist development and a newly constructed breakwater. Worth a visit to see the cathedral.

> **Approach.** Chart 188. The port lies by a low point of land with a 300 yard breakwater running due E. from the lighthouse. The approach is easy by day, and not too difficult at night. In 1967, however, the mole had been completely destroyed and the harbour was dangerous to enter. A beginning had been made on reconstruction. [Photograph facing p. 96.]
>
> **Berth.** Within 50 yards of the south side of the breakwater there are depths of 3 fathoms on a sandy bottom. Shelter is usually good; only when the wind is in the easterly quadrant is the port uncomfortable.
>
> **Facilities.** Landing at the wooden pier it is fifteen minutes' walk to the town. The shops have improved, there are good restaurants, one or two bars and a number of new hotels, all in the modern quarter, which is growing up westward of the old town.

The old town, much neglected throughout the centuries, has some admirable ecclesiastical architecture, especially the very fine Norman cathedral with an apse beautifully decorated with 12th-century Byzantine mosaics. It is said that the vessel returning from Naples with Roger II was overtaken by a severe storm; Roger made a vow that if they were saved he would erect a cathedral at the place that brought them to safety.

About 12,000 people live here and until recently were in rather an impoverished state but with progress in tourism, standards have improved. The new part of the town, built for summer tourists and consisting of tall blocks of flats and hotels, stands close westward of the old town. Club Mediterranée has set up a sailing school here.

Cape d'Orlando, whose coastal features resemble those of Cefalù, lacks the attraction of an old town and cathedral.

The new harbour built to shelter the local fishing fleet and completed nearly ten years ago is now derelict. This is the third harbour on the N. Sicilian coast set up within the last ten years to defy the northerly gales, yet all have been destroyed. Only Cefalù shows signs of reconstruction. Of the sandy waste that once formed Port d'Orlando one is reminded of the old Greek sailor's words:

> *Do not bring up here sailor: do not stow your sails because of me,*
> *The harbour you see is dry, I am but a tomb.*

In unsettled weather Cape d'Orlando has a bad reputation for squalls and heavy seas.

The mountainous coast with green belts of cultivation continues eastwards to Milazzo: the few anchorages en route are open to the north. Approaching Cape Tindaro one sees a prominent sanctuary standing above the steep cliff; behind it are the ruins of the ancient Greek city of Tyndaris which is well worth a visit; but as the nearest safe anchorage is Milazzo, it is advisable to enter that port and then drive out to Tyndaris by taxi. The prevailing winds during summer tend to blow from N. to N.E., this latter direction being maintained up to and including Messina Strait.

Cape Milazzo Anchorage or **Sant' Antonio Bay** is open only to the west. There is good holding on a sandy bottom close under the cliffs with the lighthouse bearing N.W. 6 cables. The bay is completely deserted.

Along the eastern shores of the steeply wooded Milazzo Peninsula are two monasteries, some large villas, old and new, and overlooking the port, stands the massive, walled citadel.

Milazzo is a pleasant old fishing town beside a sheltered port with an attractive quay, lined by shops and restaurants—the best shelter near the Messina Strait.

Approach. Chart 175. The citadel is conspicuous by day and the breakwater-light by night. Coming from the east, the peninsula appears like an island, the land to the southward lying very low. Tunny nets are sometimes laid out on the west side of the peninsula during the months of May and June. An oil port and refinery now occupy much of the frontage on the low-lying land east of the port.

Berth. Stern to the N.W. quay with the anchor to S.E., or alternatively, anchor in the southern part of the harbour where, except from E., shelter is good and the holding moderate on mud. The Lipari hydrofoil boats cause a lot of wash.

Facilities. Water can be obtained by hydrant near the root of the mole and from a tap 200 yards from the mole's extremity. An ice factory is 400 yards inland. There are some modest shops nearby and one or two restaurants and hotels have recently opened near the quay. Trains and buses run to Messina and Palermo. The spacious bathing beach is on the west side of the isthmus south of Sant' Antonio anchorage.

With a present-day population of 20,000, this old town, founded as Mylae by the Greeks in the 5th century B.C., has been populated throughout the ages. Nowadays tourists come here in summer both for the bathing and to catch the daily ferries which ply from Milazzo to the Aeolian Islands.

The castle, standing at a height of 300 feet, lies on a rocky elevation between the port and the sea on the western side of the isthmus. It has a wonderful all-round view over the mountain ridges towards Messina, the Calabrian coast and the Lipari Islands. Built on the site of an earlier Greek acropolis, it was occupied and sometimes rebuilt throughout the centuries successively by the Normans, Charles V, the French, and the British. It was finally besieged by Garibaldi. This was in 1860 when Garibaldi, having already routed the Bourbon forces in the country around Milazzo, found himself with what he believed to be the more difficult task of capturing the fortress. It was known to be defended by more than a thousand men, but Garibaldi had reason to suspect that their morale was low. Proof that it was so was soon provided. In *The Times* of 4th August, 1860, its correspondent described how semaphore messages from the demoralized garrison commander to the Bourbon general in Messina were intercepted by the delighted Garibaldi, who was soon in the strong position of being able to negotiate a bloodless capitulation.

THE LIPARI OR AEOLIAN ISLANDS

These steep, mountainous islands, only an hour by hydrofoil from Milazzo, average about 5 miles long; all are inhabited, the native population having a Spanish-Arab strain. The islands vary in character: one is an awe-inspiring active volcano, another has interesting archaeological remains and yet another has well-organized agriculture and mineral production. Among the foreign visitors today a proportion are keen underwater fishermen. In Roman times, according to Pliny, good quality coral used to be gathered here for shipment to the mainland towns.

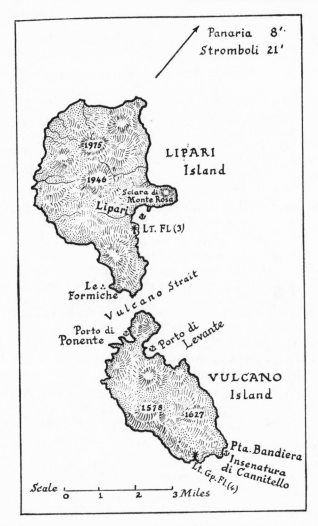

The name Aeolian was derived from the deity Aeolus, who is said to have kept the winds in a bag secluded in a cave. His inconstant character was first demonstrated by Odysseus who, after paying a call and being given a favourable wind, was blown off course beyond his objective.

With the exception of Lipari there are no sheltered harbours for a yacht, but during settled weather nearly all these islands have an anchorage affording a certain amount of lee, according to the direction of the wind. At each island a call is made by the ferry-steamer from Milazzo; Lipari and Vulcano have daily hydrofoil services with Milazzo.

Island of Lipari. The best cultivated and most civilized of the Aeolian Islands has a town of the same name.

Approach. Chart 172, plan. A yacht should make for the southern side of the massive promontory Sciara di Monte Rosa. By night there is a powerful approach light and the usual harbour lights.

Tunny nets are laid out in early summer from the S.E. projection of the Monte Rosa promontory and long-net fishing may extend as much as 5 miles to the eastward.

Berth. The substantial northern breakwater, recently lengthened and heightened, now makes conditions comfortable for yachts, which berth stern to the quay with anchor to the N.W. The outer part of the quay, reserved for the ferry-steamers, is indicated by a yellow line. In calm weather passenger-steamers prefer to berth at the quay close to the citadel, Sotto Monastero. In S.E. weather the harbour can be uncomfortable.

The hydrofoil uses the small quay by a church on the S. side of the citadel. [See photograph facing p. 176.]

Facilities. Provision shops are in the town half an hour's walk from the port where taxis are available. Ice can be bought. Fresh water, always in short supply, has had to be augmented by tankers from the mainland, and with the recent increase in tourists a tanker has to reach the island daily; sometimes a yacht may obtain a small supply by going alongside the tanker.

The ferry-steamer from Milazzo arrives daily and the hydrofoil runs a number of trips during the day.

Great progress has been made in recent years to attract tourists: two smart modern hotels have been built by the shore outside the town; there are also some more modest hotels, restaurants and a few modern shops. The quick sea communication by hydrofoil brings many daily visitors as well as more permanent ones, holiday campers and underwater fishermen.

The population of the island is now about 14,000, having declined from nearly double this number during the last hundred years. Half the inhabitants live in Lipari town which, though somewhat drab, has interesting narrow streets leading steeply up towards the citadel. This dates from earliest times, and in the Gothic palace of the bishop, which is now the museum, are imaginatively displayed some of the prehistoric and Greek finds. The cathedral, originally Norman, was largely destroyed by Barbarossa and later rebuilt by Charles V in the Spanish style. There are two Byzantine churches; but the greatest interest is the museum which should not be missed.

The extinct volcano on Mt. St. Angelo stands at nearly 2,000 feet above the sea and can be reached by a steep path passing obsidian (volcanic glass) and vast pumice quarries at Canneto; here the excavated minerals are conveyed across their own piers, to the waiting ships.

The island grows some corn which, until the present century, was entirely raised by women, who even did the grinding, harnessed to poles which turned the mill: 'Twelve female slaves the gift of Ceres grind', as Homer described them.

A sweet wine, mostly for local consumption, is also produced.

Island of Vulcano is tall and barren with a small settlement by an extinct volcanic cone. It is considered to be hardly worth visiting by a yacht.

Approach and Anchorages. Chart 172. The steep slopes of the south coast are sometimes aflame with small streams of lava. The steamer berths at the quay of Porto di Levante and sometimes at Insenatura di Cannitello on the S.E. coast where the depths are more convenient. Both these anchorages are very exposed. On the N.W. coast is Porto di Ponente, with convenient depths but open between N. and W. Long-net fishing sometimes extends 5 miles to the eastward.

Facilities. At Porto di Levante are a few modest *pensioni* and *trattorie*. There are hot mud baths and hot sea baths claimed to cure certain maladies. A daily hydrofoil service runs to Milazzo, and motor-launches ply to Lipari.

This island which first rose from the sea in 183 B.C. has a community of four hundred people who now thrive largely on the visiting hypochrondriacs who come annually to coat themselves with medicinal mud. The local people have now reclaimed for themselves a small area of flat land on which they grow vegetables.

The grand crater lies to the south; on it is Piano delle Grande Fumaroli exuding sulphur fumes which penetrate the whole island. You can climb up by following a track crossing innumerable gullies and eventually reach the rim of the crater, which has been inactive since 1890.

A few keen underwater fishermen come to Vulcano, also some campers.

Island of Salina, ancient Didyma (Twins), was so-called on account of the two conical mountain tops which distinguish it. Salina is the tallest of the group with a peak ascending to 3,156 feet. It has three villages connected by road (with a bus service) and a population of 3,500 inhabitants, mostly employed cultivating vines. A hundred years ago, a traveller described them as being 'laborious, but ferocious'.

The village of Rinella has become a centre for underwater fishing. Archaeologists sometimes come here to examine the ancient tombs and Graeco-Roman remains. Anchor off the mole only in fine weather; rocky bottom.

Island of Panaria, with a population of only about five hundred, is attractive. Outside the small town of Santa Marina the scenery is picturesque, with flowers and fruit trees.

Anchorage. One or two places suggest themselves as an anchorage: off the north of Punta Peppemaria 120 yards off shore, or alternatively off the middle cove on the S.E. shore.

141

A Club Mediterranee has been set up here. Except for the archaeological sites which have revealed Minoan influence, there is nothing here of interest.

Island of Stromboli is an awe-inspiring active volcano, often glowing red and spewing out lava to cascade 3,000 feet down its steep N.W. slopes into the sea. On the N.E. side of the island, with its more gentle slopes, is Stromboli village, whose white-washed cottages stand out against a green background of vines.

Anchorage is off the village, rather close to the shore. There is no pier, and when the steamer calls passengers are taken off to the beach by local boats. In fine weather a yacht can anchor in a sandy cove at Insenatura di Ficogrande (E. of Pta. Labronzo).

Formerly a fishing fleet was based here but, with the rapid decline in population, only two or three boats remain. About five hundred people now live in the village with its many ruined houses still crumbling as the decline continues. A track leading to the summit passes through vineyards, olive trees and bamboos. There is an occasional snake and some lizards. The last 1,000 feet is across very rough lava.

During the recent centuries many sailors in passing ships have recorded their feelings about Stromboli's volcano. One, Lieutenant Dummer, a prominent marine artist, in 1664, described this unusual sight as being 'most astonishing and terrible, and if within the hearing of the impetus the impression is inexpressible'.

The two most western islands of this group, Alicuri and Filicudi, are barren and without suitable shelter.

THE ITALIAN MAINLAND COAST
AND ADJACENT ISLANDS

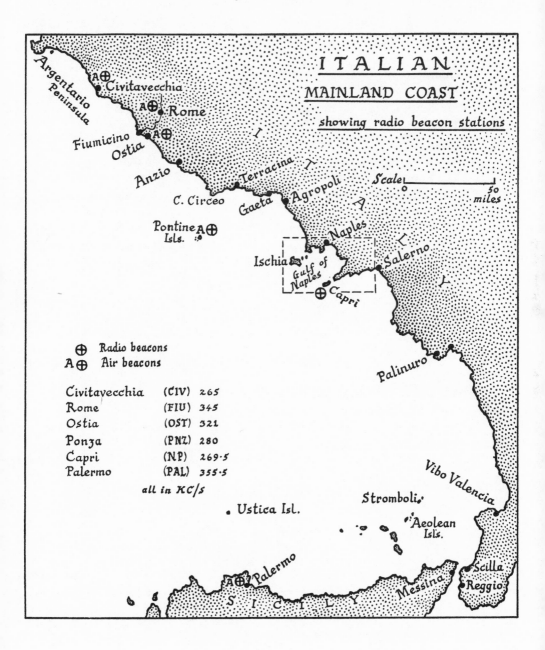

ITALIAN

MAINLAND COAST

showing radio beacon stations

Scale 0 ____ 50 miles

Radio beacons
A⊕ Air beacons

Civitavecchia	(CIV)	265
Rome	(FIU)	345
Ostia	(OST)	321
Ponza	(PNZ)	280
Capri	(NP)	269·5
Palermo	(PAL)	355·5

all in KC/s

6

The Italian Mainland Coast
and Adjacent Islands

Civitavecchia, a large commercial port without comfortable facilities for a
yacht.

Approach. Chart 1728, plan. The shoaling ledge at the extremity of the mole is marked by
a conical green buoy with a flashing light.

Berths. Yachts should go either to the Michelangelo Basin or to the Darsena Romana
entered from Michelangelo Basin through a very narrow passage. Here, among other small
craft, one may berth stern to the quay and bows secured to a buoy, or alternatively with
anchor to the west. It is an attractive place, but completely landlocked and quiet.

Officials. The Harbour Office is N. of the port. Police patrol the area.

Facilities. Fresh water is available at the quay, and shops are ten minutes' walk. Bus and
train to Rome: car-ferry steamers to Sardinia.

The port was originally built as Centrum Cellae by the Emperor Trajan who
had a villa here. It has flourished as the major port for Rome since the 13th
century and now has a population of 40,000 people. The medieval fortifications,
many of which are still to be seen, were designed by Michelangelo in 1535.

Fiumicino, a river port for small coasters supplying Rome, and also a harbour
for fishing craft. Entry is limited by a 9-foot bar at the entrance to the canal
at the Tiber mouth. Of no particular attraction to a yacht, yet it is quite convenient for a call if one wishes to visit Rome, whose great airport lies close by.

Approach. Plan on Chart 1841 and Sailing Directions. In a strong west wind the onshore
sea prevents a safe passage over the bar (9–10 feet). The two towers are conspicuous and make
the entrance from seaward easy to identify. A 2-knot current often sets westwards.

Berths:
(a) In the basin, the south side of the ruins, entered just before reaching the footbridge.
   Although very dirty, the depths here have been dredged to 13–14 feet (except at W. end).
   Here there is complete shelter and it is the best place to leave a yacht in safety if visiting
   Rome.

(b) Pass through the first bridge—opened on the signal 'S' on foghorn—and berth on the port hand.

Officials. Harbour Master and Police.

Facilities. Water is laid on to the quay the south side of the river between the two bridges and can be obtained through a hose by arrangement with the Harbour Master. (In the basin there is no water.) A market and fresh provision shops are nearby, also a restaurant and bars of modest standard. The bus service to Rome starts from the N. bank of the river over the footbridge, but the timing is erratic. Returning from Rome one should make sure of a seat by arriving in plenty of time at the bus terminal. The journey takes about three-quarters of an hour.

The River Tiber has been continually silting since Roman days, and every time a new port has been built, it has eventually had to be abandoned for this reason. Fiumicino was formed into a harbour in 1825. At that time Torre Clementina (built in 1773) stood close to the sea: today it is at least a quarter of a mile from it. The Roman Porto together with its canal built by the Emperor Trajan, is now 2 miles from the sea, which continues to recede from the advancing river-bed at the rate of 13 feet a year. The nearest that a small vessel can now get to Rome is S. Paolo, claimed to be the lighter port for the capital, but although it has two quays the channel is very narrow with depths of slightly more than 1 fathom.

One should visit **Ostia Antica,** the old port of Rome, about ten minutes by bus, where some fine mosaics of Roman trading vessels are to be seen. The great hexagonal-shaped port built during Hadrian's time to handle the Sardinian corn trade has completely silted. At that time there was a city with 52,000 people but with the decay of Rome it wilted away to a mere handful. However, once more it has become a popular summer resort.

Anzio. A useful small harbour for sheltering from N.W. winds and within easy reach of Rome. The place itself has become a summer resort, although until recent years it was a fishing port.

Approach. Chart 1728. The harbour entrance is best approached by first running in on a northerly course towards the prominent Villa Borghese. When the depths become about 3 fathoms the line of the breakwater begins to open. Then turn towards the entrance (about W.N.W.) and follow close to the breakwater into the port. Even with constant dredging the depths in the channel seldom exceed 3 fathoms, and in fresh southerly winds the seas break alarmingly on the bank just outside the port. Although local trawlers seem indifferent to these conditions, a strange yacht might think twice.

Berth either at the main quay (stern-to) or in the very crowded yacht harbour, now dredged to 2 fathoms. Good shelter inside, but southerly winds bring in a swell. It is difficult to land from a small yacht at the main quay owing to its height.

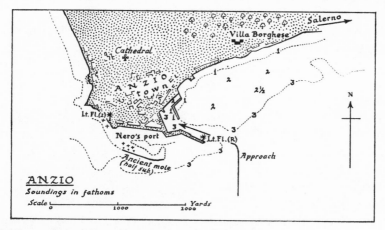

ANZIO
Soundings in fathoms
Scale

Officials. Harbour Office and Customs are by the quay.

Facilities. Shops and restaurants close by. Fresh water hydrant by arrangement with the Harbour Master. Buses run to Rome every hour, a one-and-a-half-hour journey.

The ruins of Nero's large port of Antium are usually visible some distance off as the sea is constantly breaking on the outer mole, which originally protected a harbour of about 150 acres. At the time of its construction, Antium was a popular Roman resort: Cicero had a property here; both Caligula and Nero were born here. After the Roman era the place was more or less deserted until the end of the 17th century, when Pope Innocent XII began building the foundations of the present port to shelter his galley fleet. The stonework was obtained by quarrying Nero's sea fortress on Anzio point and this material was also used to build the quay and three fortified positions at strategic points on the mole. In the centre was a fountain with several pipes 'supplying very good water'; but today the purity of water supplied by hydrant seems to have deteriorated.

Allied landings were made here during the Second World War in 1944 in order to cut German communications with Rome. In a night landing early on 22nd January a British division got ashore on the beaches N.E. of the town and an American division south of it, both landings being very little opposed. The Germans under Kesselring soon rallied, and a month later, after bitter fighting, it was feared that German counter attacks would drive the Allies back into the sea. At this time no progress had been made towards Rome, but subsequently after a build-up to 120,000 men the operation succeeded.

Leaving Anzio and making south-eastwards along the low receding coast one comes to the huge promontory of **Circeo** (1,750 feet) standing out as an island 23 miles ahead. This island of Homeric history was connected to the mainland by a swamp, and it was not until Mussolini's day that the Pontine marshes were drained to become the rich agricultural plain of today. It was here that the goddess Circe had her palace and exerted her charms upon Ulysses, delaying his voyage for a whole year. Ulysses had taken Hermes' advice— 'when Circe smites you with her wand draw your sword from your side, and spring at her as if you want to take her life. Now she will fall before you in terror and invite you to her bed—do not hesitate to accept the favours of the goddess'—Ulysses's sailors were less fortunate for some of them were turned into beasts.

Monte Circeo used to be a popular climb for visitors who ascended by a path leading to Semaphore Hill where they rested to enjoy the splendid view. On the N. side were countless ruins of Roman villas, but today, passing by sea, only modern villas and hotels can be seen; they have spread around the lower slopes, especially on the S. side. On the S.E. corner of the promontory, near Torre del Fico, a harbour has now been built.

San Felice Circeo. The new mole extends from the tower for nearly 500 yards curving in a southerly direction; a short mole from shore reaches towards its southern extremity.

> **Berth.** Either anchor in convenient depths behind the mole or secure at the new quays when completed. Harbour lights on moleheads (see *M. & P.*).

> **Facilities.** A modern resort is growing up by the port and supply facilities should be available.

Terracina, a small fishing and commercial port by the entrance to Porto Canale which, although of historical interest, is not suitable for berthing a yacht.

> **Approach.** Chart 3904. The breakwater entrance can be found by heading northwards towards the prominent supporting arches of the Roman temple of Venus standing on Monte St. Angelo. Beneath it is a large monolith of dark brown rock. The mole has a small red tower at its extremity and is lit at night; liable to silting after strong S. winds.

> **Berth.** At the root of the sea wall is the entrance to Porto Canale with a basin (having 10-feet depths) 250 yards inside. One can also berth at the outer port in depths of 16 feet or anchor outside, east of the molehead, in depths of 3 fathoms. The inner harbour is likely to be crowded with fishing craft.

The town owes its former importance to its position on the southern end of the marsh where the Via Appia touched the coast. It was the gateway to Campania, and for many years a Roman resort with large villas. The old episcopal city now stands on the southern slopes of the hill on the site of the Roman city above the new town, and has a population of about 20,000. The fine cathedral of San Cesare, built and then rebuilt from the 11th century onwards, stands on the site of the Roman Forum the pavement of which largely remains intact.

The levels and date-marks cut in the vertical rock-face by the Romans when altering the route of the Via Appia show that the sea-level has undergone considerable changes, and a century ago the declining waters left a morass which only in recent years has been drained.

Continuing eastward, the coast now becomes rather barren with cliffs and watchtowers until the massive fortifications are sighted on the point of Gaeta.

Winds. During settled conditions the day breeze usually sets in about midday, blowing gently from S.W., and then veering during the afternoon to west. It dies away at sunset, becoming calm all night. About sunrise there is sometimes a cooling breeze off the land.

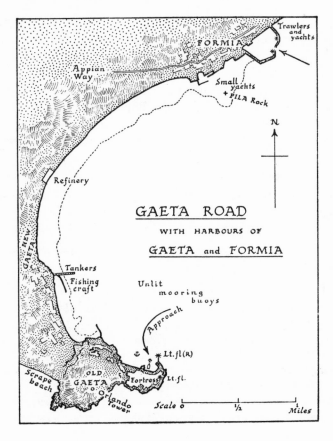

Gaeta, a fortified medieval city and ex-naval port, is worth a visit if you can find somewhere for the yacht to berth in this very congested small basin.

Approach. Chart 1728, plan. The Aragonese castle and Orlando's Tower stand out on the headland. After turning towards the S.W. corner of Gaeta Roads, a yacht should decide whether to anchor close offshore or find a berth close by the old naval arsenal. The large Navy mooring buoys in the Roads should be avoided at night. [Photograph facing p. 177.]

Berth off a small commercial quay under the fortress, close west of the naval depot. Here is excellent shelter and firm holding on mud, but the situation is far from agreeable as small coasters are continually arriving and working their cargoes. The other minor shelters are either military or a trawler port. In settled weather yachts sometimes anchor temporarily off Scrape Beach.

Officials. The Harbour Office is on the quay front denoted by a large anchor at the doorway.

Facilities. Water connection on the quay—an ice factory some distance round the bay—some provision shops, modest restaurants in the old town, but better supplies, banks, etc. are to be found in the new quarter further northwards.

Such severe damage was inflicted on the old town in the Second World War that it was not considered worth while restoring, and so the modern town has grown up further northwards round the bay; a broad motor road now skirts the shore. In the old port the 12th-century cathedral (damaged by bombs) is well worth seeing for its campanile and Roman porch; behind the high altar, in a frame, is the banner, presented by the Pope, to be flown in the Christian flagship at the Battle of Lepanto (1571). The city has endured many sieges: one in 1806 when the British navy was supporting the defending troops against Napoleon's army under Masséna; and the last in 1861 when, after 92 days, the Bourbon King and Queen surrendered to the newly-constituted navy of Italy.

Wandering round the old bombed buildings, many partially occupied by the less fortunate citizens, one can see Roman arches, columns, capitals and early masonry—all reflecting something of the city's historical past.

Formia, a new 3-fathom port close by the modern town, is used mainly by fishing craft and the Ponza–Ischia ferries.

Approach. The entrance should be approached on a N.E. course when the two small beacons at the moleheads can be distinguished. Normal harbour lights are exhibited at night.

Berth. Yachts should berth at the N.E. mole, at the inner leg which in 1967 lacked mooring rings. The outer part has underwater blocks extending up to 15 feet from the mole. The top of the mole is flat and when berthed off the inner part one can get ashore by gangplank. Shelter here is good, holding on mud in depths of 3 fathoms (2½ at the mole side). The north corner of the harbour is occupied by ferries and small freighters.

Facilities. Water and fuel at a quay near the yacht berth (15 feet alongside). There are many shops, restaurants and hotels within ten minutes' walk from the quay. The main line and the main road from Rome to Naples passes through Formia. Daily ferry service to Ponza and Ischia.

Until recent years Formia was a small seaside resort for the less rich Italians, but it has slowly grown into a large modern town without any particular interest.

Less than a mile N.W. is a small yacht harbour for shallow-draught yachts drawing not more than 6 feet. About thirty yachts can be accommodated, and there are quays, fuel and water-supply services.

THE PONTINE ISLANDS

Although there are five islands in this group, all crests of former volcanic craters, only two of them are of interest to a visiting yacht:

Ponza, an attractive island port with sufficient shelter; well worth visiting.

PONZA — View of the port looking S.E.

Approach and Berth. Chart 3904. Sailing Directions describe the entrance. In settled weather yachts berth all round the basin with anchors laid out towards the centre and sterns to the quays: but the harbour is so small that many yachts have to anchor in the bay. Although N.E. winds bring in a swell, the little harbour is normally well sheltered.

Officials. The Port Office is by the root of the mole.

Facilities. Fresh provisions, wine and many good restaurants are available by the quays. Water during the summer months is in short supply and is brought to the island by tanker. Ice can be bought from a fishmonger on the quay. There is frequent steamer communication with Gaeta and Naples. A small sandy cove close N.E. of the root of the mole provides a pleasant bathing place when the hydrofoil service is not operating.

There are sandy coves on the S.E. shores of the island where a number of yachts anchor for the bathing. In settled weather motor-boats find their way to the coves on the S.W. corner of the islet of Palmarola.

Ventotene—a quaint old convict settlement with an unspoilt village and small rock-hewn Roman galley port with all-round shelter.

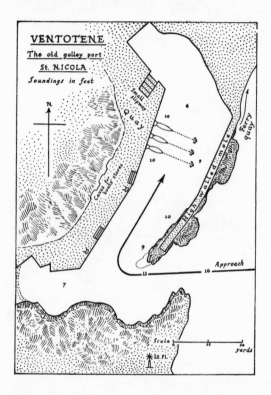

Approach. Chart 3904. The Title 'Port St. Nicola' and instructions in Sailing Directions no longer make sense. The lighthouse should be approached on a course about 260°, and then on reaching the very narrow entrance it must be entered by passing between the rocky projection by the lighthouse and another to the northward. Close inside, in depths of about 2 fathoms, one must turn sharply 90° to the N. (starboard), keeping close to the rocky shore on the *Inside* of the turn. Then proceed down the middle of the main arm of the port where the depths are consistently 2 fathoms.

In 1966 a new harbour was built immediately N. of the galley port intended largely for use by the ferry-steamers, but in 1967 some of the new breakwater had been washed away by winter storms.

Berth. Stern to the quay on the landward side where the arches in the rocks begin. Lay out the anchor to N.E. close under the breakwater. The bottom is mud, and the shelter all round.

Only with strong E. winds do the seas break over the top causing uncomfortable conditions within.

Officials. A Captain of the Port.

Facilities. Although there is a water-tap on the quay, water is scarce in summer and has to be shipped every week from Naples. Fruit and vegetables brought across from the mainland can be bought at the shops in the village at the top of the stairs on the hill. Once a week there is steamer communication with Naples, and a steamer runs to Ponza twice a week. The Post Office may be found in the same building as the Banco di Napoli. The local wine is consumed by the inhabitants of the island and summer visitors.

The island has a population of about eight hundred; it has electric power and a distillery plant. Until a few years ago Ventotene was a penal settlement, as was also the nearby island of Santo Stefano; but this, too, has recently been closed down. In addition to a few Italian summer tourists, there is also accommodation for orphan children provided by the Roman Catholic Church.

In Roman days Ventotene was called Pandataria and was first selected by the Emperor Augustus as a place of banishment for his daughter Julia on account of her adulterous behaviour. She was followed into exile by her mother Scribonia, then divorced from Augustus.

THE GULF OF NAPLES AND OFF-LYING ISLANDS

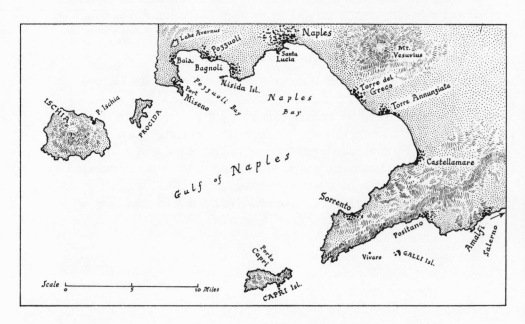

Island of Ischia
Island of Procida
  Marina
  Cala di Corricella
  Chiaiolella
Port Miseno
Baia
Pozzuoli
Bagnoli and Island of Nisida

Yacht Ports of Naples:
  Porto San Nazzaro (Mergellina)
  Santa Lucia
  Molosiglio
Commercial Port of Naples
Portici
Torre del Greco or Porto Calastro
Torre Annunziata
Castellammare di Stabia
Sorrento
Island of Capri

THE GULF OF NAPLES AND OFF-LYING ISLANDS

The small yacht and ferry ports of today are the former pleasure resorts of the Romans.

The Island of Ischia is an attractive, mountainous island, about 18 miles in circumference, with volcanic slopes richly covered with sub-tropical vegetation. Its bathing beaches and pleasant country walks have recently attracted a large number of tourists, which now outnumber an indigenous population of 32,000. There is one completely sheltered yacht port—Porto d'Ischia and one or two partially sheltered anchorages.

When populated by Greeks in the 5th century B.C. the violent eruptions and earthquakes caused the whole island to be evacuated. Later occupied by Romans, Ischia has since been renowned for its medicinal waters and its wine.

At the large *bagni* on the harbour quay one should not expect to ask for a bath as one normally would at a public bathplace or hotel. Here one must first submit to a doctor's examination and after this the operation of bathing is carefully controlled, both the bath temperature and the time one may spend in the bath. This need for caution now exercised by the authorities was realized by the Romans, but not enforced until Iasoline published a book in 1588, specifying the nature of the medicinal benefits derived from these waters and laying down rules and recommendations both for those drinking the water and bathing in it. In the whole island he listed a dozen fresh-water springs and thirty-five hot springs as well as localities of certain baths and showers. As if to emphasize the need for moderation in the enjoyment of these waters an earlier Latin inscription found inside one of Diocletian's baths reads: 'Bathing, wine and love corrupt healthy bodies; healthy bodies are produced by bathing, wine and love.'

During the last century Ischia was visited by many English travellers making the 'Grand Tour'; among those who sang its praises were Gladstone, Fenimore Cooper, the Countess Blessington and Edward Lear. Nowadays, although completely given over to visitors, the island seems less crowded than Capri. The new floating population, however, began to demand far more fresh water than was available, supplies being augmented by tankers which brought it daily from Naples. Now an underwater pipeline from the mainland provides an abundant supply.

Porto d'Ischia

The Port is worth a visit. The shelter is perfect and the scenery interesting, but nowadays it is very crowded with yachts and pleasure-craft.

Approach. Chart 1380. The correct approach course must be followed as the shoal water extends close to the sides of the channel. Ferry-steamers are continually rushing in and out of the narrow entrance. Yachts berth anywhere round the quays of the harbour with anchor out and stern to the quay. Depth here is about 3 fathoms with good holding, mud bottom, and excellent shelter all round. The only other craft that use the port are the Naples ferry-steamers which berth opposite the entrance and the wine schooners and *tartanes* which lie beside the wine stores. The harbour is apt to be very crowded.

Officials. Harbour Master's office is on the front near the steamer berth.

Facilities. Plenty of fresh provisions, and excellent white Capri wine available close at hand; there are several good hotels and restaurants. Water is laid on at the quays. Both fuel and water have recently been made available at a quay on the starboard hand when entering. Ice is brought round in a handcart or lorry.

The table wines, *bianco*, *rosso* and *roseto*, mostly grown in Ischia or on the mainland opposite, are excellent, especially '53 or '60 if you can get them. The shipyard is used to yacht work, and can haul up quite heavy craft. The hot thermal-bath establishment is close by, as well as in other places on the island. Frequent ferry services run to Naples and Capri and also a hydrofoil boat.

The best view of the harbour is from the Montagnone (840 feet) ascended by cable car, starting close S.W. of the port.

The harbour was the former Lago del Bagno and, according to Pliny, there had been a small town here before an earthquake disturbance caused it to slip away and form this lake in its place. The lake remained for many centuries until 1853 when, during the reign of Ferdinand II, a cutting was made through the narrow neck of land separating it from the sea, thus opening up the present Porto d'Ischia.

The motor road more or less follows the coast round the island, and one can make a tour inexpensively by bus. The north and west coasts are the most attractive, with pleasant coastal villages and walks through pine woods and vineyards.

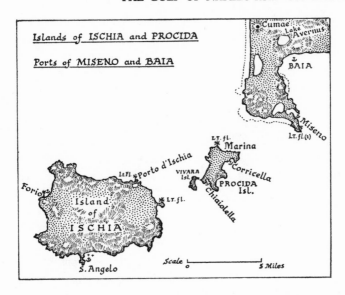

There are also one or two small harbours and anchorages with indifferent shelter round the coast, e.g. Forio and St. Angelo; but for a yacht it is often better to have the security and convenience of Porto d'Ischia and to visit the other places by land. In 1969 a new harbour was reported to be being built close east of Punta Vico on the north coast.

Island of Procida, a small and relatively low-lying island with bluff cliffs, is interesting to visit. There are two or three places where a yacht can berth:

(a) **Marina,** the main port by the village on the N. coast is distinguished in the distance by the large fortress surrounding the eastern extremity of the island. Shelter is obtained when anchoring eastward of the long mole projecting northwards from the centre of the village; but nowadays the whole quay frontage (except for a shallow section at the E. end) is monopolized by ferry craft, hydrofoils, etc. rushing to and fro so that it is almost impossible for a yacht to find room to anchor.

There are, however, alternative anchorages on the S.E. coast:

(b) **Cala di Corricella** which provides good, but open anchorage in $2\frac{1}{2}$ fathoms near the entrance to the shallow fishing port where one can land in the dinghy. When approaching this anchorage one should avoid some alarming underwater rocks lying 200 yards south of the entrance with less than 2-fathom depths.

157

The fishing village here is quite remarkable. Very old and colourful houses rise tier upon tier from the waterfront to the top of the cliff above. They are mostly buttressed with large arched doorways and windows of all shapes and sizes. The houses are painted in shades of pink, yellow and sometimes red; beneath them in the port lie the small trawlers and fishing craft, all painted turquoise blue.

At the south end of the island is the very small harbour of Chiaiolella, and the anchorage between Procida and Vivara Island (now connected by a bridge) which is recommended for shelter in strong N. winds.

(c) **Chiaiolella,** protected by two short moles (unmarked) has depths of 3 fathoms in the entrance and 2 fathoms inside, shoaling quickly at the sides. (A yacht with 6- to 8-foot draught could anchor N. of the W. mole and run out a warp.) The approach, however, is dangerous because underwater rocks lie close off the normal line of approach, and a yacht should therefore make a sweep towards the E. when actually about to enter the port.

A number of motor-yachts come here and others anchor temporarily for bathing outside the port—poor holding, weed, boulders and sand—beneath a fine red-coloured mansion. Should the wind blow from the south a yacht can anchor off the sandy bathing beach on the N.W. side.

Yacht facilities on the island are poor, but most things can be bought at Marina; the other villages have some vegetable and fruit shops, bars and small restaurants.

This little volcanic island with about 10,000 people has a personality of its own. Some of it is still hardly touched by tourism. The colourful small town of Marina with white, pink and yellow flat-topped houses, rises from the sea-front, reaching up the hill slopes to the castle on the hill in the form of an amphitheatre. In the country, dwellings are interspersed with vineyards, orange groves and orchards; the inhabitants are now more or less self-supporting, thriving on fishing, farming and boat-building. On certain fiesta occasions, the women turn out in a Greek style of costume. The old fortress, still guarded, accommodates political offenders.

Two hotels have their own bathing beach on the S.E. coast and attract Italian visitors from the mainland, but there is no atmosphere of wealth in Procida; only a few decades ago poverty forced many workers to migrate to France and South America. The surviving fine houses of the 18th century are evidence of the rich Neapolitan nobility of that period.

The origin of Procida is uncertain, but Pliny who studied early accounts of the great 5th century B.C. eruption in Ischia believed that Procida was thrown up from the sea at the same period. The island had a settled community in the Middle Ages, and history relates that in 1282 a certain John of Procida instigated the rising against the Normans known as the 'Sicilian Vespers'.* In the 16th century the Turks made several raids on Procida and in 1544 Barbarossa destroyed the whole place carrying off many of the inhabitants. Afterwards it was defended by Ciracello Castle on the S.W. corner of the island, but this was destroyed by Captain Hoste in 1806 when the French were in possession.

Entering the Gulf of Naples one soon finds that its 40 miles of coastline has little to attract a yacht; but the remarkable contrasts in the coastal formation are very striking: the bold headlands sometimes crowned with a medieval fortress, the unusual indentations and the changing character of the scenery. It seems strange to find industrial areas spreading out on the sites of Roman villas and famous early resorts. It can be a rewarding experience to follow these shores today and to compare them with descriptions by Roman writers of two thousand years ago. Although most of the attraction has gone one can envisage from these early records how most places then appeared and by identifying some of the architectural remains one can recreate a picture of certain fantastic events in Roman history.

The waters in the gulf have become so discoloured by the industrialization that many foreign visitors decline to swim, though when one passes a sandy beach it is invariably packed with Neapolitan bathers. Everywhere one seems to be in the midst of fast moving ferry-boats, motor-boats, hydrofoils and hovercraft all rushing their passengers between Naples and the two large tourist islands of Capri and Ischia. [Photograph facing p. 177.]

Port Miseno is a small inlet on the north side of the promontory with depths of about 3 fathoms as far as the inner port. The sides are bare cliffs, but the shelter can be useful for a small yacht in this part of the Gulf of Naples.

Approach. Chart 1380, plan. See Sailing Directions. Leading marks are no longer distinguishable, and a yacht should pass between the outer buoy and a stone beacon, then follow the starboard channel buoys into the port. There are 3- to 4-fathom depths before reaching the inner basin when it begins to shoal rapidly.

Anchorage. One can anchor N. of the inner starboard hand buoy in $3\frac{1}{2}$ fathoms near a temporary pier with room to swing. Some steamer wash rolls into the bay. The pier shown on Chart 1400 is military and the depths in the approach less than charted. The harbour appears to be silting.

Facilities are few—a grocer and one or two vegetable shops.

* See introduction to Sicily page 103

Miseno was named after Aeneas's trumpeter who, according to Virgil, was drowned and buried here. Augustus had the place built into an excellent harbour with three basins; at that time it was comparable with the naval port of Ravenna and became the main base for the Tyrrhenian Sea fleet. There is not much remaining today to remind one of the former naval arsenal. Entering the harbour, on the port hand, are the half-submerged blocks of the main Roman breakwater. Some remains near its root are what is left of the great summer villa of Lucullus which eventually became a royal palace and it was here that Tiberius died.

Continuing towards Sarparella Point you pass the remains of a theatre and nearby a Roman bath. Between this and the harbour were the naval barracks for the galley crews and Admiralty House, where possibly the younger Pliny found himself on the occasion of the terrible eruption of Vesuvius in A.D. 79. Some caverns in the cliffs to be seen on the starboard hand were galley stores. One of the more remarkable naval installations was that of the extensive underground water cisterns for the galley fleet. The inner basin, now the Mare Morto, is separated from the main harbour by a causeway and a bridge, and around its green slopes are a number of small modern villas.

After leaving Miseno one comes to the shores of the Pozzuoli Gulf. They are mostly built up areas alternating with modern buildings and industrial undertakings.

Baia an anchorage off the old Roman sea resort which has now become an industrial modern village with ship-repair yards and slipways.

> **Approach and Anchorage.** Chart 1380, plan. Make for a quay between the root of the mole and the harbour office; but shoal water extends for 30 feet off the edge of the quay and when berthing stern-to long warps must be used. The sunken buildings, on the seabed, which 19th-century sailing vessels were warned against, appear to have broken up.

> **Facilities.** Water can be obtained at a fountain near the root of the mole. Fresh supplies and oysters can be bought nearby.

Today Baia is partially a small bathing resort for the Neapolitans, but it is sadly disappointing after its former splendour in the days of Augustus, Nero and Hadrian. According to Horace (Epist. 1.83.) 'Nothing in the world outshines the lovely bay of Baia': but in his day the shore may have extended another 1,000 yards to seaward; the whole place was laid out as a great pleasure resort and the architecture designed for its beauty. Where the grey Aragonese castle now stands was the site of Caesar's great villa.

North of Baia towards Monte Nuovo is a low stretch of shore now bordered by the road and railway. In Roman times this had an entrance leading to Port

Sorrento Peninsula from the air

The coastline near Amalfi

The Capri coast showing the port

Julius, the naval arsenal designed by Agrippa for the Emperor Augustus. For a short period it was a busy naval shipbuilding centre, but with the ending of the Civil War at the Battle of Actium it fell into disuse and the waters of Lake Avernus gradually filled in the great port, of which only a few ruins (including some baths) remain. The surrounding country with its green and partially wooded slopes is now attractive and peaceful, but in those days the vapours of the lake were said to be so pestilent that no bird could fly across it and live. It was then an old crater with hot springs surrounded by dense forests which the ancients associated with one of the entrances to the underworld. Odysseus, Aeneas and Orpheus all used it, and it is described in detail in the sixth book of the *Aeneid*, a source which Dante later tapped for the *Divine Comedy*.

North-westward of the lake and standing on a large hilly stronghold over-looking the sea are some ruins of the most ancient Greek city of Campania. This is **Cumae** where fifty years ago archaeologists aroused world interest by finding near the gate of the acropolis, the entrance to an ancient cavern. For a while they thought they had stumbled into the approach of the famous underground retreat of the Sibyl—'a deep cave there was yawning wide and vast, shingly and sheltered by dark lake and woodland gloom' (*Aeneid*, VI, 237.8)— but further research has proved that they had unearthed a tunnel which was in fact bored for strategical purposes to provide safe road communication between the port and the sea coast at Cumae. There were actually two tunnels (built by Cocceius Anctes, the Roman engineer, who built similar tunnels at Naples), one from Lake Avernus to the Cumae Plain (where most of the city lay), the other direct through the Cumae Massif. For centuries this great fortress survived as a centre of Christianity and in the 5th century when the Byzantine Emperor came to rescue it from foreign invaders it was still considered to be, after Naples, the most important stronghold in Campania. Though disappointing today to find so little remaining of its former greatness, it is worth while making the excursion for the splendid view from the summit.

Pozzuoli, a large suburb of Naples, once residential, has now become largely industrial. No yacht would normally want to visit it except for the purpose of slipping.

Approach and Berth. Chart 1380, plan. Make for the end of the long mole extending westward from the W. extremity of the promontory. There is shelter between the moleheads in depths 9–15 feet or for small vessels in the fishermens' basin.

Facilities. Both water and fuel can be obtained at Molo Caligoliano. The local yard is used to hauling out yachts for painting.

The modern town has grown to about 52,000 inhabitants, many being employed in fishing and small industries. Known formerly by the Romans as

Puteoli, after the sulphurous wells, it was then an extension of Baia with its small port to serve the needs of the important Greek colony of Cumae. It was not until the time of Hannibal's expedition when Agrippa called for naval war preparations that Puteoli's whole existence was changed and it was soon made into a large harbour. Serving mainly the commerce for Rome, it grew into becoming her largest port with a great emporium for overseas trade, and continued for more than two centuries as an important commercial city. In Puteoli's heyday there is evidence of imports from Elba (iron ore), Spain (including rabbits—caught by Libyan ferrets—and oysters), Sardinia (corn), cargoes from Africa, the Middle East ports of Phoenicia, Cyprus and Egypt, as well as freight from India. Writers have described the excitement of the local people at the start of the sailing season when the first ships arriving from foreign lands were sighted. The city too was a centre of industry for exports: Pliny mentions the Purple factories, and the *molybdites*; there was pottery from all the local villages; the colonial merchants of Syria, Tyre, Beirut and Helio- polis had their factories here and even their temples.

The brief history of the Roman harbour can be of interest to the visiting yacht. The great engineering feat of the time was the building of the South Mole. It extended from a point S. of the present mole in a westerly direction; its construction consisted of a foundation of solid concrete formed, according to Strabo, by volcanic ash mixed with lime. This special sand ash, now called *tufa*, was known to be very durable and solid, and it was upon this that the broad quay and the arches were built. On each side of an arch was a mooring- ring for a vessel's warps. It was from the extremity of this mole that the Emperor Caligula built his floating bridge across to Baia in order to boast how he had 'ridden on horseback across the water from one city to another'. Suetonius describes the bridge as being little more than 2 miles in length. Collecting trading vessels from all directions he moored them in two lines close together by their anchors—then he had them boarded over and with earth heaped upon the planks he formed a viaduct after the fashion of the Appian Way. In A.D. 59 a distinguished traveller was brought here; St. Paul, on his way to Rome, arrived in an Alexandrian ship named *Heavenly Twins* (after the figure-head), and according to *The Acts* (chap. XXVIII) 'after a day in Rhegium a south wind sprang up and we reached Puteoli the next day'.

It may be wondered why so little is known of this Roman port, especially in these days of skin-diving and aerial survey. Photographs taken at 1 to 2 yards distant reveal nothing of value to the surveyor, and in the clouded water divers find it difficult to work effectively but certain features of the port have recently come to light. The thirteen columns and arches of the South Mole and some drums of columns by the present shore line were discovered nearly two centuries ago. It seems that on the west side of the bay the original shore line and its built-up quays now lie nearly half a mile to seaward and are submerged at least 2 fathoms. The seabed which began to rise in the 2nd century A.D. eventually reached a height of 16 feet, but now it is back to the original level, although tending to rise again. There have also been irregular disturbances of the seabed.

We know something of the unloading basins described by Strabo and of the great Ripa market (158 feet by 127 feet), still to be seen (partly submerged) in the present town. The harbour lost its importance in the 2nd century A.D., not only due to the destruction of the mole, but because the long haul of cargo by road to Rome became no longer economical, and so Ostia came to be built instead. The population slowly dwindled away; but the city of Puteoli had once seen great days. It had the third largest amphitheatre in the Empire, libraries, an academy, many medicinal baths, and the sumptuous villas of prominent Romans, including Cicero and Sulla.

When Puteoli was sacked in the Middle Ages some of the columns and masonry were used to build the cathedral.

Bagnoli and the Island of Nisida. Bagnoli is a small industrial town with two long mineral-loading piers extending from ashore. The area between these piers and the small mountainous island of Nisida is a sheltered anchorage.

> **Approach and Anchorage.** Chart 1380. There is no difficulty in finding this anchorage, for the short mole extending from Nisida Island is lit. Anchor on mud in convenient depths.

The shores of Bagnoli are now fully industrialized and of no interest. It is connected by a causeway to the steep-to little island of Nisida. On the island is a small circular cove which was once the side of a volcano; it is now shallow and out of use. Nisida was the Nesis of the Romans, where Brutus and Cassius initiated their plot against Caesar; also where Brutus took leave of his wife, Portia, before setting off for the Battle of Philippi, the news of which subsequently caused her to commit suicide by swallowing burning coal. This small island once served a helpful purpose for British warships, when in 1860 a hospital was set up to deal with a smallpox epidemic. This disease was spreading fast among the ships' companies of H.M.S. *Hannibal* and *Renown*; but by segregation and hospital nursing it was eventually brought under control.

Beyond Posillipo are the **yacht harbours of Naples,** Porto San Nazzaro, Santa Lucia, and the Molosiglio basin. All are very crowded and make it almost impossible for a strange yacht to get a berth. The best choice is Santa Lucia, for here it is sometimes possible to find a most convenient—though highly expensive—berth. Should no berth be available at any of these harbours one must either make for Ischia or seek shelter in one of the small commercial ports, Portici being the nearest.

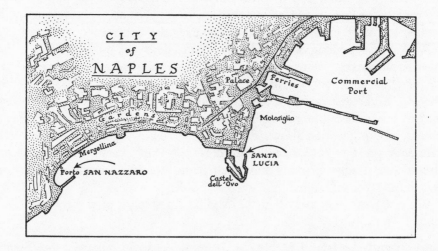

Porto San Nazzaro or **Mergellina,** which has been deepened, now accommodates some deep-draught yachts, a few small ones and the hydrofoil terminus.

> **Approach.** The entrance is approached in a S.W. direction. The larger yachts are berthed stern to the rough mole, some twenty being accommodated.
>
> **Berth** off the mole if possible, bows N.W. The landward side of the harbour which is shallow has some room for small yachts and also the hydrofoil landing quay.
>
> **Facilities.** The dinghy is necessary to get ashore, but there the place is far from shops and the city centre. The district is known as Mergellina.

Santa Lucia, the most convenient yacht port for Naples, lies close S.W. of the commercial port under the old fortress of Castel dell'Ovo.

> **Approach.** Chart 3931. One can make for Castel dell'Ovo and then turn up between the channel buoys into the entrance.
>
> **Berth** wherever there is room—stern to the quay. The harbour is always crowded.
>
> **Officials.** Harbour Master, Yacht Club Italia and Canottieri Savoia.
>
> **Facilities.** Water is laid on to the quays, where there is also a number of expensive restaurants. Fuel and ice can be got at the small garage on the S. side of the port. Hotels are nearby and it is only a short walk to the city where everything is to be obtained. The Club makes a high charge for berthing in Sta. Lucia. English Calor Gas cylinders can sometimes be filled, while you wait, at 'Gas Butano', Via Argine 245 (Tel. 35 26 75). This is at the S. end of town near the start of the Autostrada to Pompeii.

Castel dell'Ovo and Santa Lucia yacht harbour

The castle which dominates this small port was built on the site of a former Roman villa and stands out prominently.

Note: If Sta. Lucia is full a yacht should make for San Nazzaro or decide upon another course of action as previously suggested.

Close N.E. of Sta. Lucia is the small yacht port, **Molosiglio.** There are depths of 12 to 15 feet, and a dozen large yachts are usually berthed at the S. mole, smaller ones opposite. This little harbour is always crowded and it is unlikely that a strange yacht could be accommodated.

The Commercial Port of Naples is entirely occupied with steamer traffic, and there is no possibility of a yacht finding a berth inside.

The City of Naples (Napoli), with 1¼ million people, requires a guide-book if making a stop of more than a couple of days. For a brief stay it is suggested that both Herculaneum and Pompeii should be visited, and the Museo Nazionale in the city itself. Here are antiquities recovered from Pompeii, from Paestum and Herculaneum, many of them by Greek sculptors and brought by sea from that country. The Aquarium is also worth seeing.

The present commercial port is of recent construction, but a small port existed many centuries ago. The Arsenale de Marina built by Mendoza in the 16th century had a 500-yard mole and, according to 1805 Sailing Directions, 'a fine high lighthouse'.

The old port could hardly have witnessed more exciting scenes than those which occurred in the winter of 1798. Only a few weeks after the Victory of the Nile, the military situation in Italy had deteriorated and Nelson had to warn the King of the Two Sicilies that he might have to vacate Naples and proceed to his second capital in Sicily. The British fleet at this time was unfortunately scattered, watching other ports and on blockade duties, and as December wore on, Nelson, alone with only his flagship at Naples, had decided

165

that the 22nd must be the day of the evacuation. Meanwhile, for some weeks, the royal party and the British residents, who were also to go, had been busy packing their belongings—the Queen in particular had been sending daily to the Hamiltons at the British Embassy cases of treasures labelled 'Stores for Nelson' (these were assessed by Nelson to be worth 2½ million sterling). To carry all the stores and baggage Nelson had three transports and, for the evacuees, his flagship *Vanguard* later joined by a brig; also a Portuguese warship which, he wrote, 'counted for nothing'.

The molehead at which frigates could normally berth, was not to be used on account of the uncertain political situation. Had the forts rebelled it was thought they might well have turned their guns on the ships, and so all the vessels were anchored well offshore, rolling heavily in the swell on the evening of 22nd December. Ship's boats under Nelson's personally written orders assembled at Vittorio landing stage at Molo Giglio to embark the royal party with the Hamiltons and court attendants. To provide against surprise action no detail in the boatwork had been overlooked: Nelson ordered every boat to have grapnels, men were to be armed with cutlasses, a soldier escort, emergency signals and so on. The royal party brought down by Nelson from the Palace through the secret tunnel was embarked with difficulty into the heaving boats which then had a half-hour's row through the swell to *Vanguard*. On board they began to settle down for the voyage when it was discovered that the royal baggage had found its way to other vessels. The second party consisting of the Neapolitan knights and the main British contingent fared worse: they were put on board the Portuguese warship where conditions were described as chaotic. However, on the evening of 23rd December, *Vanguard* weighed and, taking with her the brig and twenty merchantmen, sailed for Sicily. 'Next day,' wrote Nelson, 'it blew harder than I have ever experienced.' Early on the 26th they entered Palermo and berthed behind the mole. Soon after 9 a.m. the King disembarked: 'Manned ship and cheered him until on shore', was the last recorded entry in *Vanguard*'s log on completion of her royal mission.

Mount Vesuvius. Since earliest times Mount Vesuvius has dictated the destiny of the coastal towns which sprang up in Graeco-Roman days round the Gulf of Naples.

Today, Vesuvius is a quiet truncated cone standing at about 4,000 feet above sea level, and rising at an angle of only 10 degrees on its lower and middle slopes. Until a few years ago the popular route up the mountain was by Thomas Cook's railway which took one quite near the edge of the crater. This has now been superseded by a well-graded road to carry tourists by bus or taxi to a point above the observatory where a magnificent view of the sea and mountains makes the ascent well worth while. The trip takes a good three hours and to reach the top one must employ a guide. There is also a chair-lift which takes one to the edge of the crater.

In Roman times during the reign of Augustus this volcano was as quiet as it is today, but Neapolitans had a rude shock in Nero's reign when the mountain came to life with a fearful earthquake, damaging much of Herculaneum and Pompeii. During the next few years there were more earthquakes, and in A.D. 79 occurred the furious eruption which overwhelmed Pompeii, Herculaneum, Stabia and other coastal resorts. On this occasion the uncle of Pliny the Younger, then commanding the galley fleet at Misenum, set sail to carry out rescue work. The elder Pliny went across to Stabia to make scientific observations, and lost his life by suffocation from the fumes. Similar violent manifestations have since been recorded: one in A.D. 471, when the wind is said to have carried showers of ashes as far as Constantinople.

In more recent times it is often forgotten that in 1906 Vesuvius became very active for nearly a year, culminating in Naples being plunged into complete darkness and a hundred people killed while east of the mountain the whole countryside was devastated. The last activity was in 1944 but this was not of such a serious nature, although villages on the slopes were destroyed and ash was carried as far as Bari.

Movements of the earth's crust at places around the shores of the Gulf of Naples still continue, and during historical times a number of variations in the sea-level have been recorded.

Information on the following ports might be useful in event of necessity, but the places are not recommended for a visit.

Portici is a dull little commercial port with a 200-yard mole extending in a W.N.W. direction. A yacht may find good shelter at the quay on the inner side, but after strong W. winds the entrance is liable to silt.

Torre del Greco or **Porto Calastro** is a fishing harbour with a small town.

Approach. Chart 1380, plan. In normal weather the approach is easy but dangerous in S.E. winds. Although the harbour suffers from silting, one may normally expect 2½ fathoms inside.

In the eruption of 1631 this little place suffered severely, the lava from Vesuvius sweeping down into the sea and accounting for 3,000 of the inhabitants. Today the village is known for its coral ornaments and cameos.

Torre Annunziata is a large and usually empty commercial harbour affording good shelter except from S.E. It is unattractive and unsuitable for yachts.

Approach and Berth. Chart 1400, plan. There is a wide choice, but the inner mole is probably the best: lay out anchor to the E., stern to the quay. Harbour dues are charged.

This harbour, now used for discharging grain, is 2 miles from Pompeii, (bus every twenty minutes); but if specially wishing to visit Pompeii, it is preferable for a yacht to lie at Santa Lucia and make the longer journey by road.

Castellammare, the ancient Roman Stabiae, has become a large commercial port with naval dockyard, as well as a summer resort. The plan on Chart 1400 illustrates the lay-out of half a dozen stone piers with quays, and a number of mussel-beds.

The town of about 35,000 people spreads itself along the waterfront, and is of little interest to a visiting yacht. The Roman town of Stabiae, destroyed in the great eruption of A.D. 74, lay to the N.E. As there are a number of Italian towns named Castellammare, this one is distinguished by its official name of Castellammare di Stabia. In the Napoleonic wars the dockyard was used by British warships both for careening and for making limited repairs. After the flight of the King and Queen of Naples when British and Allied troops were holding southern Italy, this port was used for landing supplies, and when in 1806 evacuation became necessary, British forces were taken off from here.

Sorrento, a pleasant, though rather unsheltered harbour (with a short mole) off an attractive coast.

Approach and Berth. Chart 1400, plan. The large Hotel Victoria standing on the cliffs is conspicuous—a yacht can anchor in depths of 2 to 3 fathoms off the hotel bathing beach. Shelter from the day-breeze is effected by the mole, but this is largely monopolized by the ferry-boats and local craft. From other quarters this anchorage is exposed.

Officials. Customs and Harbour Master.

Facilities. Most things can be bought in the town—a zig-zag ascent of twenty minutes; but the place is disappointing. There are large hotels and restaurants in the town, and one or two cheaper ones in the port.

Although quite clean for bathing, one would not wish to come here for a special visit.

Sorrento was the Roman Surrentum, so named because it was thought to be the place where Odysseus resisted the call of the Siren.

Island of Capri. This small, mountainous island, well known to many tourists visiting Italy, is very attractive and of great historical interest. Unfortunately its small and crowded harbour can be very uncomfortable for a yacht. [Photograph facing p. 161.]

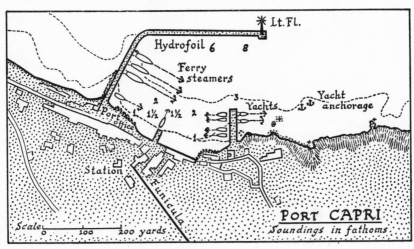

The Port

Approach and Berth. Chart 1400, plan. A yacht should proceed to the shoreward end of the mole and find a berth, stern to the quay, clear of the ferry-steamers. The harbour is very disturbed by the wash of the hydrofoil and the ferries which are constantly coming and going.

Officials. The Harbour Master's Office is near the root of the mole.

Facilities. Provisions are available at shops close to the quay. Water for the island has to be supplied by tanker daily, and one may obtain only small quantities from a tap with the Harbour Master's permission. A funicular takes one up the hill to the piazza, whence buses ply on tours round the island. Ferries and a hydrofoil run frequently to Sorrento and Naples.

The island, a great lump of limestone rock, has mountains of more unusual and attractive form than anywhere in Italy. The town of Capri stands on the saddle between the precipitous hill of Anacapri (1,600 feet) and the steep mountain on the east. Visitors to the island today know it largely because of the Blue Grotto, Axel Munthe's *San Michele*, Gracie Fields' villa at Marina Piccolo, and stories of the orgies attributed to the 'libertine emperor' Tiberius.

(a) The famous Blue Grotto was only discovered at the beginning of the last century, and its fame was spread around the world by German and other western writers and eccentrics who at that time had begun to settle in Capri. This grotto soon became more widely known than the former Grotta Oscura which was destroyed by a landslide only a few years previously. Inside the grotto can be seen traces of a flight of Roman steps descending for 20 feet beneath the present surface of the sea, thus proving that since Tiberius's time the subsidence of the island is considerable.

(b) *San Michele* is a villa built into the fabric of a former Roman dwelling on the mountain slope by Dr. Axel Munthe, the Swedish writer, during the eighties of the last century. His purpose was to display objects recovered from ancient sites, on the walls and in the garden of the villa; later, tourists could see something of the legacy left by the Romans. His book, *The Story of San Michele*, still has a world-wide readership.

(c) Gracie Fields' villa at Marina Piccolo was built in recent years and has attached to it a public bathing place with a swimming pool which many tourists, now driven from the over-crowded piazza, flock to visit. Buses run every half hour during the day from the piazza; thus the place is crowded by day but deserted at night. In settled weather a yacht may anchor here in depths of 4 fathoms on a sandy bottom. The best berth can be found by approaching to a position between the cliffs and on a line formed by projecting seawards the rocks at the base of which the restaurant *Delle Sirene* stands.

(d) Stories of the orgies of Tiberius have been enlarged upon in recent years, and are taken from the histories compiled by Tacitus and Suetonius, written more than a hundred years after the emperor's death in A.D. 37. Tiberius was actually close on seventy when he finally settled in Capri. Modern historians discredit these stories, believing that the emperor has been much maligned.

Before Tiberius settled here, the place had been made fashionable by Augustus, who came to live in his sumptuous villa after the Battle of Actium in 31 B.C. There is evidence that he collected for decoration specimens of huge fossilized bones 'saide to bee of gyants'. Subsequently, this villa and many other dwellings were all destroyed during the centuries when Capri had no significance; but early this century a local doctor and naturalist, Ignazo Cenio, while excavating at Quisisana near the site of the villa, dug up large paleolithic remains which proved that ancient man had inhabited this island possibly half a million years ago.

During the 17th century, Capri was the seat of a bishop whose See amassed much wealth from snaring and then selling the migratory quails. The men at this time were either shipwrights or seamen in the Spanish galleys. During the Napoleonic Wars, after the King and Queen of the Two Sicilies had already fled to Palermo, Capri was occupied by France. It was, however, re-captured by the British under Sir Sidney Smith (of Acre fame) and held for two years until 1808 when Sir Hudson Lowe (later keeper of Napoleon at St. Helena) again lost it rather ignominiously to the French. The French attacking force brought with them long ladders, seized from the lamplighters of Naples, upon which they scaled the cliffs and soon overcame British resistance. This spirited enterprise is commemorated by the word 'Capree' on the Arc de Triomphe in Paris.

As a popular place of residence Capri seems to have attracted eminent foreigners rather than Italians. An early visitor at the end of the 18th century was Lady Hamilton. Describing her visit to an elderly and somewhat untravelled Italian prince living in Naples, she was astonished at his hazy idea of the geographical position of Capri; in a subsequent letter to Greville she wrote '. . . he asked me if I had been there by land—only think what ignorance! I stared at him and asked him who was his tutor.' In the last century a great number of foreign poets, writers and painters settled on the island, of whom Norman Douglas is probably one of the best known. Nowadays the island is completely given over to tourism.

After leaving Capri for the mainland the beautiful mountainous coast, often called the 'Amalfi Riviera', continues in an easterly direction as far as Salerno, where it then trends S.E. towards the toe of Italy. [Photograph facing p. 160.]

The Galli Islets or **Isole Galli.** These somewhat uninspiring rocky islets lie about one mile off the southern shore of the Sorrento Peninsula. Galle Grande, the largest, is 1½ miles south of P. St. Elia and is covered in shrubs, with a tower and a villa near its centre. The other two islets are about 200 yards distant on either side.

These were the islands of the Sirens whose voices sounding across the waters brought many mariners to their doom. When Ulysses passed, having plugged the ears of his crew with wax, he made them bind him head and foot to the mast, where he remained until the temptation had passed.

When the Argonauts came, and Orpheus sang from his ship *Argo*, the Sirens, overcome by his alluring voice, are said to have flung themselves into the sea and were turned into rocks.

There are no anchorages or suitable landing-places at these islets.

Positano, a small attractive town with an open anchorage in the bay, is often used by yachts in settled weather during the day.

The town stands on the steep hillside above, and in summer is crowded with visitors who pause here for the restaurant and the view during their coach tours which follow the winding road round the coast.

More than three centuries ago the place was strongly fortified, but after being captured and sacked by the Pisans it never recovered. It became an unimportant fishing village until the recent decades ushered in the tourists who have deprived it of its charm.

Amalfi. A picturesque little town in a mountainous setting with a small, insecure harbour at the foot of a deep ravine.

Approach. Chart 1400, plan. Coming from the south the place is difficult to discern; but sometimes the cemetery, appearing on the hill as a number of superimposed terraces, is conspicuous. [Photograph facing p. 161.]

Berth. Yachts berth stern to the quay but at an angle, with the anchor laid out between N.E. and E.N.E. In settled weather this harbour is pleasant, but in the event of a falling barometer and Sirocco winds one should never leave the boat unattended. After the southerly swell the wind may shift to the north and become a *Tramontana*, when violent squalls descend from the mountains which can severely damage a yacht against the quay. In this eventuality there is room for a small or medium-sized yacht to swing to an anchor in the centre of the bay.

Officials. The Harbour Office is near the root of the mole.

Facilities. A water hydrant is on the quay. There are a number of good hotels, restaurants and shops, which in summer, are usually crowded with tourists who usually bathe off the shingle beach inside the harbour. The local wines are similar to those at Capri and Ischia.

Despite the tourists, Amalfi with its 6,000 inhabitants, is most colourful and attractive. It is difficult to imagine this small town in Crusading days eight

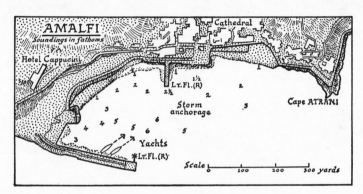

hundred years ago when it was a powerful city-state of 50,000 inhabitants rivalling even Pisa and Genoa. Her mastery at sea was such that her maritime law was accepted by the majority of nations trading in the Mediterranean.

The small crescent-shaped port enables one to see most of the surviving old buildings from the yacht: the fine cathedral in Lombard-Norman style is still beautiful, although it was largely reconstructed early in the last century. The four-storey campanile, with the Greek columns from Paestum supporting the cupola, was built six centuries ago. The famous bronze doors, remarkable for the delicate work of the reliefs, came from Constantinople and are said to be 11th century work. From the same city came the body of their patron saint, St. Andrew, which lies in the crypt.

Near the Piazza del Duomo is the statue to Flavio Gioia, the first European to make use of the Mariner's Compass which he had brought from the East. In honour of the King of Naples the fleur-de-lys was placed at the head of the compass rose instead of the letter N.

Another building which attracts the eye is Amalfi's smart hotel. It stands prominently on the hillside west of the town, and is in fact a 13th-century building, the former convent of the Cappucini. Between periods of disuse this building has also been a hostelry and a naval college. A famous landmark no longer remaining is the tower which imprisoned the innocent Joanna of Aragon—heroine of the famous Elizabethan drama *The Duchess of Malfi* by John Webster.

One should hire a car and drive 4 miles up the steep Iragone valley to Ravello, an old and beautiful hill village with a remarkably fine cathedral and other classical buildings.

Salerno is a large commercial port of no interest to a yacht.

> **Approach.** Chart 1361. The port entrance is difficult to find by day, the distant objects being not easy to discern. The castle on the hill and the peak San Liberatore are referred to in Sailing Directions. Nearing the port the small lighthouses on the mole extremities—white with either red or green bands—stand out more clearly.
>
> The breakwater has been lengthened in a S.W. direction. On entering the harbour its mole should be followed closely towards the root until clearing a shoal marked by a small black buoy.
>
> **Berth** on the W. side of inner harbour, stern to the quay of Molo Ponente.
>
> **Officials.** The Port Office is at the N.E. corner of the port.
>
> **Facilities.** There is no provision made for yachts. The relatively large town is close at hand, and here with a choice of many shops, hotels and restaurants, one can find most requirements.

Although there is a record of King Manfred extending the port as early as 1260, it was not until this century that the large modern port was constructed. It now supports a town population of 136,000. The cathedral, a fine 12th-century building, founded by the Norman Robert de Guiscard, was built of the columns and stonework which the Romans had added to the Greek temples of Paestum. Except for the beautiful bronze doors and the 12th-century pulpit there is nothing to merit a close inspection of the interior.

Salerno has had a medical school for nearly a thousand years and is said to have inherited from the Greeks the teaching of Hippocrates.

Agropoli Bay affords open anchorage during settled weather if one plans to visit the Paestum temples.

> **Approach.** Chart 1842. By day the old town on the high promontory is conspicuous, but the castle and towers referred to in Sailing Directions are not always easy to discern.
>
> **Anchorage.** According to the yacht's draught, it is convenient to anchor 50 to 100 yards off the end of the stone pier on a bottom of thin weed or sand. The depths appear to be slightly greater than those charted. One can land in the dinghy on the N.E. side of the pier on a beach of packed seaweed.
>
> **Officials.** A Customs Office is situated in the N.E. corner of the bay, and Ship's Papers should be presented when landing.

Facilities. Provisions, ice, etc. may be bought in the town nearby—a dull little place of 8,000 inhabitants.

One must hire a taxi and drive northwards for 8 miles to the three Doric temples of Paestum (*Poseidonia*) which are probably the finest examples of early Greek architecture in the whole of Italy, including Sicily, and the largest of

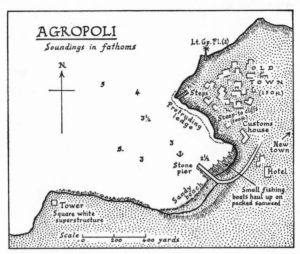

them is claimed to be the most perfect Doric temple in existence. Dating from the 5th and 6th centuries B.C., the temples lie on the coastal plain close to the sea. It seems strange to see them standing alone without a sign of the original forum, theatre and treasury which before the silting of the river according to Strabo, all formed part of this great trading port. The original town founded by the Sybarites had already sunk in importance during Roman days when the surrounding country was known only for its beautiful roses. The buildings of the town were plundered in the Middle Ages; only the marble facings survived to decorate the cathedrals at Amalfi and Salerno. But the temples remained to be of service to mariners, for the Genoese continued to show them on their charts as prominent seamarks for vessels approaching the coast.

> 'The pilot Palinuro cried aloud
> What gusts of weather from that gathering cloud
> My thoughts presage. . . .'
>
> VIRGIL, *Aeneid* V., trans. Dryden

Palinuro, a useful port of refuge in event of deteriorating weather, and a pleasant port of call at other times.

Approach. Chart 1842. Sailing Directions give an accurate description as to the use of this anchorage in emergency.

Anchorage. Anchor in 6 fathoms about 70 yards from the western shore of the bay. The holding on a sandy bottom is good. A new quay extends for about 170 yards along the waterfront by the hillside. Fitted with rings and bollards it is intended mainly for the fishing craft with which it is often crowded. No space is reserved for yachts, but one might be fortunate in finding a berth here.

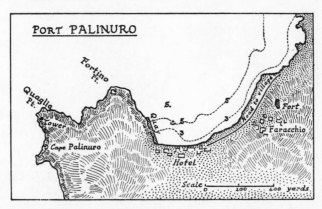

In event of strong winds it is advisable to run a warp to the rocks and lay out a kedge to steady the ship's head. Although the wind will not blow home, the anchorage is subject to strong gusts of short duration. The force of the sea is broken by Fortino Point, but a swell is reflected from the cliffs which is at its worst when the wind blows itself out on N.W. A stern anchor is sometimes a help.

Facilities. Fuel and water, as well as plentiful supplies can be bought in Palinuro village, 1 mile distant, along a new motor-road. Near the coast a number of villas and a small hotel have grown up; simple supplies can now be obtained by the port, and there are two good restaurants nearby.

Palinuro was named after the helmsman of Aeneas's ship who, after falling overboard, was washed ashore and then murdered by the natives. The entrance is remarkable for the steep protecting promontory standing 656 feet above the sea; it is flat on top, with ruins of the fort, still a visible reminder of the former importance of this anchorage.

In 1811, when England was at war with France, two British frigates, *Imperieuse* and *Thames*, arrived off the entrance in the evening of a November day. They had seen enemy ships sheltering within, and having already gathered an assault party of two hundred and fifty soldiers from Messina, landed them, together with marines, to capture the fort on the heights. Against strong French opposition they fought their way up; but the old tower, which is still to be seen, was so strongly defended that the fort could not be captured until the frigates

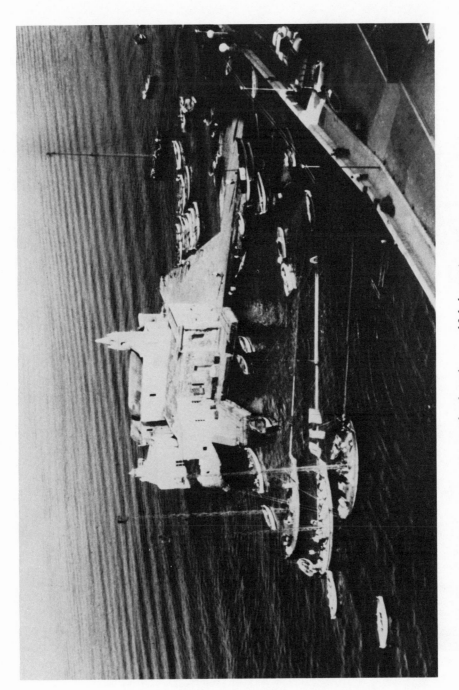

Lipari Island with swordfish boats in port

The Gaeta Peninsula from the air

The Bay of Naples

first moved in to bombard it. When this had been achieved the British force remained in possession of the heights for two days, blowing up the ramparts and hurling the captured guns into the sea, while the frigates brought away six gunboats, twenty-two feluccas laden with oil and twenty large spars.

Close southwards of Palinuro a point of land projecting from the coast partly shields the **Bay of Camerote** from N.W. winds. Here a small harbour with suitable depths is reported as now being built.

Following the long stretch of coast south-eastwards from Palinuro towards the Messina Strait most yachts keep away from the coast and make direct for one of the Messina ports, about 120 miles distant. Should a yacht be overtaken by bad weather from the north she can claw under the coast and choose one of the following fishing ports for shelter:

Meratea, a small recently built harbour, lying half a mile S.E. of St. Venere Tower. (See *M. & P.*)

> **Approach.** The port may be found by steering for the hillside village with its distinctive campanile. Above the mole may be seen a few houses standing at the head of the cove—two vertical lights are exhibited on the molehead at night.
>
> **Anchor** as convenient or berth off the quay.

Cataro, a small fishing port about 1,500 yards S.E. of Cape Testa with a mole (about 150 yards long) extending from a hook of land in a S.E. direction and protecting the seaward flank of the port. The mole's extremity is lit at night. (See *M. & P.*)

> **Anchor** as convenient off the sandy shore or berth off the quay, but the S.E. corner of it is reported to have silted. (See *M. & P.*)

If, during a yacht's southward passage, the wind should suddenly shift to the S.E. and freshen to a Sirocco gale the best course for a yacht is to return to Palinuro.

In the **Gulf of St. Eufemia** is a long sandy beach backed by a plain with the anchorage off St. Eufemia village, and at Pizzo; both are partially sheltered by a concrete pier or mole. The Plain of Maida is of historical interest, for it was here in 1806 that General Stewart with 4,700 men inflicted very heavy casualties and completely routed a large force of Napoleon's army. The victory was celebrated in London and gave its name to the new suburb of Maida Vale.

Vibo Valencia Marina is a small fishing-commercial port, well sheltered and, though pleasant, is of no particular interest.

Approach. Chart 140, plan. Proceed into the western corner of the harbour towards a new quay.

Berth. Let go in about 5 fathoms and haul in the stern to the quay which is rather high to be convenient. The shelter is claimed to be good under all conditions except the *Gregale*.

One may also anchor in the S.E. corner of the harbour near some fishing craft (on moorings).

Officials. The Port Office is near the head of the harbour between the two moles.

Facilities. Fresh water can be obtained from a tap with hose on the quay near the Coast Guard vessel's berth, by a white buoy. Some unexpectedly good provision shops are nearby, and also a market. There is a restaurant and trattoria close to the quay. An ice factory is only 30 yards from the berth recommended. The main railroad from Rome to Syracuse passes the town—eight hours to Rome.

The main town for Vibo Valencia lies over the hill. This is at Monteleone, with its castle built by Frederick II, and a population of about 10,000. The port has a couple of thousand inhabitants employed mostly in the cement works, in the port installations and in fishing.

Scilla, a useful place to shelter or bring up for the night when close to Messina Strait.

Approach and Berth. Chart 177. There is no difficulty in entering the harbour, day or night: the famous whirlpool of antiquity is hardly noticeable today. A convenient berth may be found a little more than half way along the quay, letting go the anchor in about 4 fathoms on shingle; anchor with ship's head about S.S.E. and haul in the stern to some steps at the steep quay. The holding is poor, but except in N.E. weather shelter here is claimed to be good.

Officials. Both Police and Military sometimes wish to see a yacht's papers.

Facilities. The poor fishing village by the harbour has very few supplies to offer; but there is also a village on the S.W. side of the promontory.

The high mole with the quay makes one feel very shut in, and the rocky shore on the landward side does not add to the attraction. However, with a choice of only Reggio or Messina at hand one can do worse than choose Scilla for a night anchorage, especially if the tidal stream is to be considered.

The harbour is used by swordfish-boats during the season. Standing on the top of the steep-to promontory above the harbour is the castle. In the 1908 earthquake this was destroyed together with the town of Scilla and a large proportion of the 5,000 inhabitants, many of whom were then occupied with the silk industry. Exactly a hundred years before this tragedy occurred a small British force had occupied this castle and held it for eighteen months as a thorn in the flesh of Napoleon's occupying force in Calabria. Supplies were landed on the beach beneath and in the Second World War some of the Italian army being evacuated from Sicily was also landed here.

After leaving Scilla a yacht has the choice of either making a Sicilian cruise (see Ch. 5) or of continuing through the Messina Strait and then heading east-wards. If the decision is to head eastwards then two alternatives are open: the

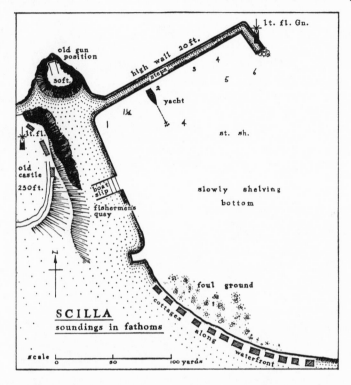

straight sea passage to the Ionian Isles of Greece or the coastal route to the Adriatic.

Making for the Adriatic one passes under the heel of Italy, crossing the Gulf of Squillace (Squalls) towards the large Gulf of Taranto. The monotony of the mountainous shores is broken by occasional small villages lying at the foot of conspicuous mountain torrents, which from seaward appear as broad flowing rivers. This wild, inhospitable Calabrian coast presents a complete contrast to the more gentle coastlines of the Tyrrhenian Sea.

> *There is pleasure in the pathless woods,*
> *There is rapture on the lonely shore,*
> *There is society, where none intrudes,*
> *By the deep sea, and music in its roar:*
> *I love not man the less, but Nature more.*
>
> BYRON, *Childe Harold's Pilgrimage*

7

Yacht Repairs and Laying-up

Although French and Italian yachts which visit the Tyrrhenian Sea prefer to winter in their own countries, other yachts—and especially the British—now make use of the facilities provided at Malta.

Italian yachts occasionally make use of the yard at Ischia, and many winter here afloat, especially if they have permanent crews living on board; however, when they require work to be done which cannot be done by their own crews they usually head for the few first-class yards on the mainland. If slipping only is needed this can be done effectively at Pozzuoli or at the Cantiere Navale Postiglione, Via Posillipo 34, Mergellina, Naples; but while there are many small building yards turning out standard-type craft throughout Italy, and a number of fishing-boat repair yards, there are very few yacht yards on the Italian coast capable of carrying out yacht work with skill and efficiency. Probably the best-known yard in the Tyrrhenian Sea is at **Porto Santo Stefano.** At Cantiere dell'Argentario yachts are hauled up and stored for the winter. They are not laid-up afloat in the port. Hauling-up is by the skid-cradle method but a Patent Slip is shortly to be built. Storage charges are calculated on the area occupied by the yacht. To store under cover costs about 40 per cent more than in the open. The yard undertakes repair work and has a staff of shipwrights, engineers etc. The standard of yacht fittings, especially in stainless steel, is high.

In 1968/69 the cost of painting a yacht prior to launching was based on a charge of about £1 per man-hour.

MALTA

Malta. This historic island with its naval associations is now independent within the British Commonwealth. No longer a naval base, it now caters for yachts and in the winter of 1967/68 about two hundred and twenty yachts chose Malta for laying-up, the number increasing year by year.

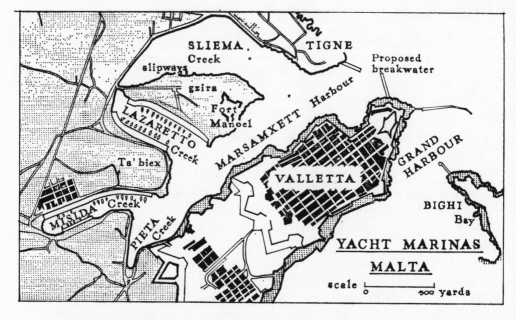

Plan showing the quays at Lazaretto and Misida Creeks where yachts are berthed.

Approach. The heights of Valletta which divide the two harbours may be sighted at a great distance when approaching from the northward. On arrival a yacht should proceed straight to the Marina in Lazaretto creek.

Berth. At a serviced quay at Lazaretto Creek (south side) about 60 yachts can now be berthed stern to the quay. 5-ton sinkers and anchors hold a chain (trot) at convenient distances from the quay, to which 'risers' in ¾-inch chain are attached to buoys for easy berthing of yachts up to a maximum of 140 feet in length. There are also other arrangements for larger yachts.

On the opposite shore at Manoel Island similar berths for yachts have been arranged, and today on the sides of Misida Creek the quay has been built up and yachts can now be accommodated here. This is the most sheltered place during winter gales (*Gregale* N.E.). Although shelter at Lazaretto Creek is normally good, a strong easterly wind may bring up a swell, and one should therefore ensure that a yacht is not left unattended. To improve the shelter in the port plans for building a breakwater at the harbour entrance have been drawn up, and recently extensive model tests were carried out in research tanks.

In 1968 a crane to lift medium-sized yachts was erected near the slipways and a place cleared for storing yachts during winter.

No harbour dues are charged, but in 1969 a berthing fee of 5*d*. per foot per week was asked, and 9*d*. per foot per week when laid up ashore.

Officials. Customs, Health and Police may visit a newly arrived yacht. The main offices of these officials is at Grand Harbour, but their sub-office is in Lazaretto Creek.

The Royal Malta Yacht Club, open only on race days, is on the east side of Sliema Harbour.

Facilities. At the Marina, water, telephone and electricity (240–120 voltage a/c) are provided at normal rates. Fuel can be bought both 'duty paid' and 'in bond'; twenty-four hours' notice is required and the vessel must proceed to sea within twenty-four hours of receiving it. Fresh provisions can be delivered daily, and dry provisions can be obtained at wholesale prices to the value of £5 or more. Wines and spirits obtainable from Saccone & Speed, Simonds Farsons and Captain Caruana may be bought 'in bond' within twenty-four hours of the vessel sailing; Customs officers will seal them on embarkation.

There is a good bus service between the Marina and Valletta.

The Government Officer responsible for the Marina in 1967 has an administrative office at Gzira.

Laying-up and Refitting. The following agencies for yachts have been set up:

(a) Ripard, Larvan & Ripard, Ltd., 156 Coast Road, Ta'Xbiex, Malta.

(b) Yacht Services (Malta) Ltd., 165 Ta'Xbiex Coast Road, Ta'Xbiex, Malta.

(c) Camper & Nicholsons (Malta) Ltd., 49 Royal Court, Ta'Xbiex, Malta.

The main business of these firms is looking after unattended yachts during the laid-up period, and arranging for them to be fitted out in the spring.

The most important matter for the owner of an uninhabited yacht to ensure is that in event of a *Gregale* some responsible person is immediately available to get on board and look after the yacht. Firms make a fixed charge for their services (calculated on the vessel's length—i.e. so much per foot overall) per week for attending to warps, washing down, airing through, pumping bilges, attending to batteries and engine and keeping the boat clean. All other work, i.e. varnishing, painting, re-rigging, caulking, engine overhauls, etc. which is undertaken against specific written instructions, is costed on a time basis. They are also able to arrange for yachts to be slipped for routine bottom cleaning and painting or repair. Surveys can also be undertaken in conjunction with Lloyds Agent.

There is Manoel Island Shipyard and a number of engineering shops at Marsa. The Patent Slip on Manoel Island, inherited from the Admiralty, has been converted to commercial use especially for yachts, and is operated by Malta Docks, a subsidiary of Swan Hunter Ltd. They haul up 3 yachts at a time and undertake to scrub and coat with two coats of anti-fouling (owner's purchase) at a cost of about £60 for a medium sized yacht, plus a daily rental of £2 10s. (1968). A small amount of repair work can also be undertaken, but skilled labour is short and costs about 12s. to 15s. an hour.

Services of a sailmaker, carpenter, rigger and engineer can be obtained at the Marina. Admiralty charts at Smith & Co., Christopher Street, Valletta.

Gas cylinders can be filled and supplies of Italian Butane and Pippi gas can be obtained in their own cylinders.

In January 1969 it was announced from Malta that the sum of £8 million was to be spent on the further development of Manoel Island as a marina. When completed it is anticipated that 1,800 yachts can then be accommodated at Malta.

Transit Stores. Imported paint, cordage and hardware stocked in the shops is a little more expensive on account of freight and import tax. However, the more expensive and specialized yacht stores may be obtained by air from abroad as transit stores and these can be collected and cleared through Customs by one of the agents. At Malta, synthetic fibre rope, hemp and sizal rope may be purchased fairly cheaply through the agents as there is a good factory now in operation in association with Tough of U.K. Good marine paints are also available, made by a subsidiary company of Hempels. Fuels and lubricants of the well-known brands are easily obtainable.

General Information. Although Maltese government notes are used, English notes are negotiable.

There are many places of interest including archaeological sites within easy reach by car or bus.

The months of August and September can be very hot.

A number of modern hotels have very recently been built and the standard of restaurants has improved.

There are daily air flights to London, a regular steamer to Syracuse and a bi-weekly sailing to Naples.

The *dghaisa*

The ubiquitous *dghaisa*, in use for many decades in the Valletta harbours for carrying ashore officers and libertymen from ships of the fleet, has now dwindled to very small numbers. Usually crewed by two men, standing to their work and facing forward, these boats move swiftly. Passengers embark always at the bow of the *dghaisa*, while she is held steady at an angle to the quay or ladder by the bowman. When the fleet sailed on a training cruise each battleship or cruiser would carry one or two *dghaisas* with their crews, and one of the events at every regatta was a spirited *dghaisa* race on which there was heavy betting among the fleet.

Index

Figures in italics indicate references to maps